. . . and there was light

JOHN CAPON

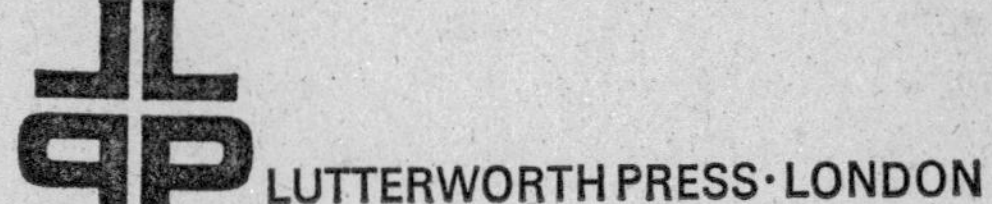

First published 1972

ISBN 0 7188 1936 5

Printed in Great Britain by
Hunt Barnard Printing Ltd., Aylesbury, Bucks

CONTENTS

AUTHOR'S NOTE

THIS BOOK was virtually completed within three months of the events it records – not, perhaps, such an unusual feat in these days of instant publishing but still an achievement which, as a full-time working journalist, has meant that I have done nowhere near as much research on the subject as I would have liked. May I therefore apologise in advance to any whose contribution to the Festival of Light may have been overlooked or under-emphasised.

I am grateful to all those who have given me information for this book, in particular the two organising secretaries of the Festival and other Executive Committee members, but I must emphasise that the views expressed in the book are entirely my own.

My thanks must also go to my publisher, who having suggested the book in the first place kept the pressure on at just the right level, and to my wife, who not only managed the typing of the numerous tape transcripts, the rough draft and finished manuscript, but also contended with the demands of a strident two-year old and an expected "happy event" round about publication day of this book.

I approached my task as a Christian journalist broadly in sympathy with the aims and intentions of the Festival as I understood them but with little foreknowledge of what lay behind it. In tracing the story of the Festival from its earliest beginnings and setting it in the context of the early 1970s, I hope that those who were involved in it during the hectic days of last summer may perhaps relive the experiences they had then. I hope, too, that some who may have been uncertain about the validity of the Festival and sceptical of its effect may read this book and thus be better informed as to its strengths and weaknesses and better able to assess their own attitude to what must by any standards rank as one of the more remarkable phenomena of our time.

JOHN CAPON

December, 1972 REDHILL

Part One

Chapter One

SEEING THE LIGHT

As the cross-channel steamer pulled into Dover harbour on a grey November afternoon in 1970 for Peter and Janet Hill it was virtually the end of the last lap of a journey that had taken them 8,000 miles through eleven countries.

They had left India where they had been working as missionaries for four years and travelled by Volkswagen through Pakistan, Afghanistan, Iran, Turkey, Greece, Yugoslavia, Bulgaria, Austria, Germany, Luxembourg and Belgium. The car belonged to their travelling companion who was a Swedish missionary, Erik Jallen, and *en route* they made several interesting contacts in the Moslem and Communist countries where they were able to leave much-needed Bibles. Jallen was going on to Sweden so he dropped Peter and Janet in Brussels.

At Ostend they joined the boat which was to take them on the last stage of the journey across the water to their homeland. It was a rough passage, with the rain coming down in torrents. As they talked excitedly of their forthcoming reunion with friends and relatives the white cliffs of Dover came into view, and within a short space of time the boat was reversing, with some difficulty, into Dover harbour. After the briefest of customs' formalities when the boat docked they were soon embracing their family and friends. The family party crowded into two cars, and set off through the harbour gates into the town of Dover itself.

As they were driving through Dover Peter looked up at a huge advertisement hoarding dominating the street. He saw the sort of poster that people in Britain had come to take for granted. It portrayed a shapely, attractive, scantily-clad girl proffering a pint of beer. Commonplace it may have been to the average Briton but it hit Peter Hill squarely between the eyes. Four years in India might have dulled his recollections of British life and practice but he was sure he had seen nothing quite like it on public hoardings when he was last in Britain in 1966.

Shortly afterwards he went into a newsagents to buy a newspaper and as he searched the shelves for the one he wanted it seemed as though almost every magazine he looked at had a nude, or semi-nude girl on the front. He looked around. He had not stepped into a pornographic bookshop by mistake. It was a perfectly respectable newsagents with people milling around buying this and that, and yet there on the bookstall were magazines selling sex in a way which he thought four or five years ago would surely have been carefully hidden away out of sight. It was the same with the newspaper he bought. It seemed to be openly condoning, even encouraging sexual behaviour which he felt sure would not have been so commended in the mid-1960's. What had happened during his four years away? Was all this now regarded as normal? Was he abnormal to react in this way?

Had he known it, his experience had been shared dozens of times by people returning to Britain after periods of a few years spent in a foreign country. They too had reacted with shock and dismay at the marked change in public attitudes to sexual morality which to those living in the middle of the situation had gone almost unnoticed, as one convention after another was broken and barriers were removed. Few people realized that in the last five years hard-core pronography had come out from the Soho back-streets and was being sold openly in suburban bookshops; the comparatively mild titillation in films had become aggressively raw and explicit perversion; the current affairs and drama departments of the broadcasting media worked on the basic premise that a straight-forward marriage relationship was now no longer the "norm", and sexual explicitness was acceptable family viewing.

Peter Hill, therefore, was not alone in his reaction or his

concern; many others who like him had recently returned from abroad felt the same way. But he was to discover that there were yet more people, many of them committed Christians, who had not been overseas but had stayed in Britain and become convinced that moral standards were being undermined by various forces at work in society. They had watched it all, thinking themselves powerless to halt the gathering momentum of the swing towards sexual permissiveness. In 1971 they found their voice, and led by Peter Hill and others of similar persuasion they filled Trafalgar Square, challenged the government, the media and the Church, and mobilized a mighty army marching for the Light.

* * *

Two out of Peter's four years in India had been with Operation Mobilization—usually abbreviated and described as OM. In the months to come this twenty-nine year old man was to be described in the British press as a "missionary" and while the term is not inaccurate it is important to note that OM is quite unlike normal missionary agencies. Founded by an American, George Verwer, OM has become a movement harnessing the energies of young Christians (mostly from Britain and America) on a sort of "Voluntary Service Overseas" basis. Every year thousands of students and others are "with OM" engaging in enthusiastic work in many countries including their own, distributing Christian literature. In four years in India Peter and Janet—as with other OM workers—had "lived by faith" receiving no regular salary. Peter's plans for his furlough in England included a considerable amount of deputation speaking. He hoped to enlist more support for his work in India before returning, but as he travelled around the country speaking at meetings he was increasingly conscious of the "moral landslide" he had noticed immediately on his return. He found this trend was evident also in young people's thinking, and however urgently Peter spoke about the needs of India he kept coming up against the challenge of the needs in Britain.

There had been times in the past when he had given himself to periods of prayer and fasting, and during December of that year he set aside a week when he was free from other responsibilities to fast and meditate and pray. He had about six different items which were engaging his attention as he prayed, when suddenly, without premeditation, he had a vision of tens of thousands of people, many of them young, marching for Christ in London and "taking a stand for righteousness". There was some "opposition", he remembers, in the shape of "something black trying to move in on the side of the march", but it was "absorbed into the whole thing". He describes it quite clearly as though he were watching a television screen, though the vision lasted for only a few seconds. He was immediately concerned to know what he should do. He felt that God might be calling him to take some part in a demonstration such as he had seen in the vision, but he was equally certain that his call was to India. The needs there were so great and the number of available workers so few compared with the abundance of Christian workers and leaders in Britain. He turned once more to prayer and asked God to give him three confirmations of this vision if he was to go forward and take up the challenge.

Within a day or two he happened to pick up a magazine in which one particular sentence seemed to "click" with what he had experienced. The writer was saying it was time Christians united together and did something positive for Christ.

Still unconvinced and conscious of the enormity of fulfilling the vision he had received, he and Janet attended a Prayer and Bible Week at Ashburnham Place in Sussex during the first week in January. It was about this time that the then Anglican Bishop of Blackburn, Dr. Charles Claxton, organized a March of Witness through the city by about 10,000 men calling for higher moral standards and witnessing to their Christian faith. Those present at the Ashburnham Conference decided to send a telegram to the Bishop expressing their support and sympathy with the demonstration. Here was Peter's second confirmation.

Then one of the leaders of the conference, Campbell McAlpine, stood up on the platform and said how wonderful it would be if what had happened in Blackburn could happen in London. Almost as though describing what Peter had seen, McAlpine mentioned a possible rally in Trafalgar Square or Hyde Park and a March of Witness. Here was his third confirmation, and as they had their time of prayer that day he recalls that he was "trembling a little" because he felt that God was speaking to him, urging him to share his vision with the group. This he did, and several people prayed that such a demonstration might take place. Someone also told of a vision which had been given to Mrs. Jean Darnall, an American who together with her husband, Elmer, ran the Christian Life College, an interdenominational Bible school at Poole, Dorset. She had seen the country clothed in blackness like a thick blanket followed by the appearance of a light in one place and then other lights appearing in different parts of the country and gradually linking up with each other and streaming towards London.

When Peter heard of Jean Darnall's vision he felt he had all the confirmation he needed to take action along the lines of his vision. He was quick to realize that to organize a demonstration on this scale would require a large amount of professional assistance and voluntary help if it was to be a success. As if by way of immediate confirmation Don and Maggie Barnett, youth workers in London's East End, came up to him after the prayer session and offered him hospitality and a telephone in London anytime he needed it, an offer he was subsequently to take up. He approached several of those present at the Ashburnham conference to talk the matter over. It was in conversation with Denis Clark, an evangelist who lived in Worthing, that Malcolm Muggeridge's name first cropped up. "If you were to get someone like Muggeridge involved", he said, "half the country would come." He did not know it at the time but in fact Malcolm Muggeridge lived only a few miles from Peter's home in Eastbourne. But how should he go about making contact with someone of his standing?

He left the conference still uncertain as to the course of

action he should take. For the next few weeks he was fully booked with deputation meetings, talking about India. Then at the beginning of February he went to see Eric Hutchings, the Eastbourne evangelist, for whom his wife Janet had worked at one time. He told him of his vision and of the way God had seemed to confirm it to him and as he spoke Dr. Hutchings pulled out a radio script which he had broadcast on his *Hour of Revival* radio programme the previous October.

"I preached on this very thing last year," he said, "that Christians should be marching for Christ."

After further discussion he assured Peter that he would stand behind him in any plans that might subsequently be made and gave him the telephone number of the Rev. Eddy Stride, rector of Spitalfields in London and formerly a vicar in Dagenham. Stride had a reputation as something of a trouble-shooter in the Church of England. A former shop steward and a keen trades unionist he had written a weekly column in the *Church of England Newspaper* for twelve years. During that time he had also made his presence felt as a member of the Church Assembly, the governing body of the Church of England now replaced by the General Synod. During the latter part of 1970 he had been taking an increasingly strong line against pornography and had been involved in several well-publicized protests, including one with Lady Jane Birdwood and others at the final performance of the play *Council of Love*, which contained scenes of blasphemy and explicit sex which shocked even some of the hard-bitten London theatre critics.

Stride came straight to the point. "This has got to be political," he said. "It has got to be in Trafalgar Square because that's where political things happen."

Peter Hill's next series of meetings was in Birmingham where there was considerable interest in the work he had been doing in India.

"If you're going to Birmingham," said Stride, "You ought to see David MacInnes and Mary Whitehouse."

The Rev. David MacInnes, precentor of Birmingham Cathedral, was a young evangelical Anglican clergyman who had been closely connected with the work of the well-known London City church, St. Helen's, Bishopsgate. He was in great demand as a speaker at student conferences and missions. Mrs. Mary Whitehouse had come to fame some six years previously when she had started a Clean-Up TV Campaign. An art teacher with responsibility for sex education, she had been appalled at the effect of television programmes on the girls whom she taught and had tackled the broadcasting media rather as David tackled Goliath, but with growing support from all sections of the community during the late 1960's. Although ridiculed and pilloried by the liberal-intellectual fringe the National Viewers and Listeners Association, which she founded, had made a responsible contribution to the raising of broadcasting standards.

Peter Hill made an appointment to see Mrs. Whitehouse and expounded his ideas to her.

"We've been praying for something like this for two years," she said, but added that she was unable to give much assistance as at that time she was heavily committed to writing her book, *Who does she think she is?* which was published towards the end of 1971. She, too, thought that Malcolm Muggeridge would be an enthusiastic supporter of the venture.

Muggeridge's conversion to Christianity, one of the most widely publicized of recent years, had taken place slowly, and because of his standing in the world of the media he has had a ready platform from which to proclaim his new-found Christian faith. He did so with characteristic sharpness, adding his own curt rebuke to the masters of the media for the way in which they were leading the "present Gadarene slide into decadence and godlessness". But Muggeridge was out of the country at that time and there was no immediate opportunity to sound him out for his support.

Peter Hill returned from Birmingham armed with a list of names and addresses from Mary Whitehouse, the full support of David MacInnes, and the growing awareness that whatever was going to be done needed to take place before the end of the year. Late September seemed a possible time and so the date of September 25, the last Saturday in the month, generally seems to have been in the centre of people's thoughts from then on. For the next few weeks Peter continued to travel around the country speaking at meetings on India, but wherever he could he took the opportunity to sound out individuals he met about the possibility of a nationwide witness for Christ.

One of the names Mary Whitehouse had given him was that of Mrs. Polly Bennett, of South Woodford, secretary of one of the most lively and active branches of the National Viewers and Listeners' Association in the South-East. Peter arranged to go and see her to talk about the project. As it happened the local VALA committee was meeting at her home the same day, so Peter was able to talk to them as well. The chairman of the committee was Colonel Orde Dobbie, son of Lieut. Gen. Sir William Dobbie an outstanding Christian military leader who distinguished himself in the defence of Malta during the Second World War. Col. Dobbie had retired from military service and become Secretary of the Southwark Council of Social Service in London. He questioned Peter about the project very closely and seemed satisfied with the answers he gave, as were the VALA committee who offered all possible support.

The following day Peter had lunch with Gordon Landreth, General Secretary of the Evangelical Alliance and shared the whole project with him. On all sides now he was receiving encouragement to go forward and it was clear that if something was to happen that year plans must soon be drawn up to handle all that would be involved by way of organization and publicity. On March 10, he spent virtually the whole day in the Barnett's home with the telephone, checking on the various contacts he had made during the preceding weeks to satisfy himself that it was right to go ahead. He arranged a preliminary meeting for those who had shown a major interest in the project, among them Jean and Elmer Darnall, Eddy Stride, Col. and Mrs. Dobbie, Gordon Landreth and Nigel Goodwin, a freelance evangelist and a professional actor deeply concerned to relate Christianity to the arts.

They met at the headquarters of the Evangelical Alliance in Chelsea at lunch-time on Wednesday, March 17, to discuss what was called, for want of a better name: Project About Moral Pollution—or Project AMP as it was known. (Just four days before they met, a retired missionary from Japan was spending her customary hour a week praying for Britain when she "had a strong impression of young people marching to Hyde Park". It was not until much later that she heard about the outline plans for just such a march which were to be drawn up within a few days of her time of prayer.) Sharing a sandwich lunch they discussed plans for mass rallies in London on September 25 linked by a March of Witness, together with regional activities held in as many provincial centres of population as possible.

Ever since Peter Hill's first contact with Eddy Stride and in all subsequent discussions with other people, the project had been thought of as having a twin purpose – to protest against "sexploitation" in the media and the arts (referred to increasingly by the rather euphemistic term "moral pollution") and to proclaim the Christian Gospel as the positive answer to it. It was natural that some of those present at the meeting were particularly concerned to make a civic or political protest against moral pollution, whilst others emphasized the potential for presenting the claims of Christ in an evangelistic context. Clearly, not all those who it was hoped, would support the first objective would necessarily support the second, and it was therefore felt important to have two distinctive and separate rallies, together serving the twin purpose envisaged. That the two should be linked by a March of Witness was the obvious fulfilment of Peter Hill's vision.

The first meeting broke up before discussion of the various issues had been completed so those present agreed to meet again two days later. By the time they had adjourned after the second meeting they had hammered out a basic structure for the organization, involving a Council of Reference, an Executive Committee and several sub-committees to handle such matters as prayer, finance, public relations, each of the London rallies, co-ordination of events outside London and other related activities. They had also prayed a good deal about the project together. In fact it was to be a feature of all the subsequent meetings of the group (which became the Executive Committee) that a large proportion of their time in committee was taken up with prayer.

Drawing up a Council of Reference proved something of a problem. The idea behind it was sound enough. So as to encourage support from the whole of the Christian Church the committee wanted the names of well-known and respected Church leaders and prominent figures in public life who would give the project a degree of authority and commendation. It was important that it should not be thought that the project was simply the brain-child of a minority group, unrepresentative of the Church at large. The fact that Gordon Landreth, of the Evangelical Alliance, was involved with the project from the start was a considerable help in this respect, but names for the Council of Reference still came in slowly.

Col. Dobbie, the provisional Chairman of the Executive Committee, was asked to produce a Statement of Intent which could be circulated to regional church leaders and others who might be interested in the project. There was still dissatisfaction with the provisional name, but no readily agreeable alternative was forthcoming. "Campaign for Clean Living" was one suggestion discussed at committee meetings, but did not find general approval.

One of the first collective actions of the committee was to urge people with whom they were in touch to write to Lord Longford voicing their support for a speech he was to make in the House of Lords on April 21 expressing his own concern at the increasing amount of pornographic material circulating in the country. A liberal-minded Roman Catholic peer, he had been a member of the Cabinet in the past Labour Government and was a keen advocate of penal reform. He announced in the Lords that he was setting up an unofficial commission on pornography. (Though it seems difficult to believe from the press coverage subsequently given to him, that was the first occasion on which he was publicly associated with any protest against pornography.) Peter Hill subsequently saw Lord Longford at the beginning of May to share the project with him and received his warm support.

At the end of April the committee, which had been meeting weekly since mid-March decided to have a month's break during which Peter Hill could get on with the basic groundwork for the project without the necessity of reporting back to the committee. Accordingly, the next meeting was fixed for the end of May, by which time the whole project had taken several major steps forward. The first step was that Malcolm Muggeridge became actively involved. On his return to this country, Mary Whitehouse telephoned him and mentioned Peter Hill's visit to her. Muggeridge expressed interest and Mary Whitehouse told Peter to get in touch with him. They met on a Sunday afternoon at the end of April and immediately established a good working relationship. As Peter outlined the plans Muggeridge's eyes lit up.

"It's a Festival of Light" he said, and so the name was born.

Nothing further came from their discussion except that Muggeridge agreed to talk about the project with some of his influential friends and also agreed to his name going on the Council of Reference.

On Monday May 17, the Rev. John Bickersteth, of Ashburnham Place, called to see Peter Hill on his way home from a conference in Dorset with an idea which had been discussed there concerning the project, namely, the lighting of beacons on hilltops throughout the country to symbolize a warning to the nation. (In the summer of 1588 a chain of eighteen beacons was lit on strategic hills from Plymouth to London and from London northwards to Yorkshire to warn the nation of the approach of the Spanish Armada.) The next day Malcolm Muggeridge telephoned to make the same suggestion and the day after Peter called in to Hildenborough Hall to see Justyn Rees, son of the late Tom Rees, well-known evangelist who had planned a massive campaign for the autumn of 1970 entitled Time for Truth. When he died earlier that year the campaign had been cancelled, but one of the events which they had proposed in connection with it was the lighting of beacons along the Armada line. Several of those who had planned to be involved in the Time for Truth campaign had already linked themselves with the new project and it seemed natural that the ideas from the former should be considered in connection with the latter. Indeed Peter was given all the names of those associated with Time for Truth in view of the close affinity between the two projects.

That evening Peter was booked to speak in South Woodford, where he had first met Col. Dobbie. After the meeting he returned to the home of the Rev. Gordon Snelling, minister of Walthamstow Baptist Church, who subsequently agreed to act as prayer secretary for the project. Later that evening the telephone rang. When Peter answered it a voice said, "I'm Steve Stevens".

* * *

Steve Stevens had been a familiar figure in evangelical circles during the preceding seventeen years as home director of the Missionary Aviation Fellowship, an organisation which provides small aeroplanes for the use of missionaries in remote situations overseas. He had become involved in the work of MAF when he resigned his commission with the South African Air Force. (He was born in Britain but went to South Africa with his family when his father, an army officer, retired.) He had been awarded the Distinguished Flying Cross for his work with the Balkan Air Force Group over Yugoslavia during the Second World War and was later a pilot on the Berlin Airlift. He joined MAF in 1950 with his wife Kay (from Johannesburg) whom he married in 1947, and pioneered the mission's work in the Sudan for three years. They came to Britain when ill health struck them both at the same time, Kay had a severe haemorrhage during pregnancy and Steve lost the sight of an eye through a detached retina caused by extreme heat and exhaustion. Originally only intending to stay for three months in order to get "the best medical treatment in the world" for Steve's eye, they remained in England both fully involved in the work of the Missionary Aviation Fellowship for the next seventeen years.

In 1955 they purchased a house at 37 Eastwood Road, South Woodford, the ground floor of which became the headquarters of MAF. The first year Steve took up the reins the MAF income was only £1,000 per year. When he gave up the job at the end of 1970 the income had grown to £60,000 per year. It was clear that with such expansion of the work larger premises were needed to house the headquarters organization and several unsuccessful attempts were made to find alternative accommodation. Eventually an old mission hall was found nearby which could be partitioned into office accommodation, and it was finally agreed that the MAF offices should be vacated during the month of May 1971.

During the time that Peter Hill was first sharing his vision with other Church leaders, Steve and Kay were in the United States. When they returned from their three-week stay in the middle of March, Kay was thrilled to hear about Peter Hill's visit to the VALA committee meeting earlier in the month. She had been active with Polly Bennett in the work of VALA for the preceding two years, helping at meetings, urging action on permissiveness in the media and circulating material to all those concerned about the decline in moral standards.

Shortly after their return a petition was to be presented at No. 10 Downing Street expressing support for a Birmingham GP Dr. Robert Browne, who had hit the national headlines when he was found not guilty by the Disciplinary Committee of the General Medical Council of professional misconduct for telling the parents of a sixteen year old girl that she was taking the contraceptive pill. Dr. Browne, a member of an Elim Pentecostal Church in Selly Oak, had made it clear that he regarded his action as morally justified, but there had been widespread criticism of his decision. As Kay Stevens came away from No. 10 she was handed a copy of the first Minutes of Project AMP, and was immediately heartened to see they included the names of Gordon Landreth, Col. Dobbie, Eddy Stride and Nigel Goodwin.

She noted the date September 25 mentioned in the Minutes and subsequently mentioned it in correspondence with others urging them to contact Col. Dobbie. Essentially an active woman, she began to get rather restive as the weeks passed and nothing appeared to be happening in connection with the project. With the date of September 25 looming ever closer she realized that an enormous amount of work and effort would have to be put in if it was to be a success. By the middle of May she had still heard nothing and was beginning to think the project would never get off the ground. Then her daughter Pam came home one evening from a house meeting she had attended locally at which Peter Hill had spoken, and Kay decided to act.

She persuaded Steve to 'phone Peter there and then to find out what was happening. As a result of that 'phone call Peter and Gordon Snelling went to visit the Stevens. One of Peter's growing concerns at this time was the provision of some sort of office for the Festival in London. It was becoming clear that he was going to need substantially more than a bed and a 'phone in London to handle the arrangements for September 25. Steve and Kay had a quick conference together and immediately offered the use of one large room as an office on the ground floor and another as a bedroom for Peter and his wife. The committee accepted the offer gladly and so it was that 37 Eastwood Road became the London headquarters of what was to become the Nationwide Festival of Light. It was in an ideal situation, within five minutes of the station on the Central Line of London's Underground (half-an-hour from central London) and within 100 yards of bank and post office.

When MAF moved out of the ground floor the accumulated wear and tear of several years was revealed and Kay set to with vigour to repair the damage and make the premises as attractive as possible. Unfortunately this coincided with a period during which she became unwell and was ordered by her doctor to lay off work for ten days or so. Ignoring his advice and trusting in God for strength she set to with a will and redecorated almost single-handed the entire ground floor. The first room to be done was Peter and Janet's bedroom, which fortunately was quite small, but the other rooms were big with high ceilings and time-consuming walls.

Having offered his home as a headquarters Steve was inevitably drawn into the organizational pattern of the Festival. He fully sympathised with its aims, having been a member of the local VALA committee for the previous two years. He agreed to help the Festival, therefore, in a part-time capacity in the first instance, but it soon became clear that the amount of work involved would require something more like full-time assistance.

By the time the next committee meeting was held on May 26 he had been offered and had accepted the post of joint secretary with Peter Hill. A treasurer had also been found, Michael Greenwood, a City businessman, as had two new committee members, Paul Cunningham, London advertisement manager of the *Cambridge Evening News*, and the Rev. Don Irving, representing the Church Youth Fellowships Association; but they were still without a recognized chairman. Sir Frederick Catherwood had been approached but was already heavily committed to Lord Longford's Commission on Pornography. The Council of Reference comprised only six names so far: Bishop Goodwin Hudson, Lord Longford, Malcolm Muggeridge, Professor Robert Boyd, Cliff Richard and Mary Whitehouse.

A decisive committee meeting took place on June 2, this time at the Spitalfield's rectory of the Rev. Eddy Stride in London's East End. The biggest attendance so far, fourteen people, thrashed out several basic questions which had been hanging fire during the intervening weeks since the committee first met. To everyone's relief the name of the project was finally agreed. It was felt that Malcolm Muggeridge's original suggestion on hearing of the project was the most positive and attractive. Accordingly the project was officially designated the Nationwide Festival of Light. After some discussion it was agreed that the committee was responsible for organizing and directing the whole Festival, but that the detailed work would be done by sub-committees reporting back to the main committee.

The final draft of a Statement of Intent was considered. Originally prepared by Col. Dobbie, it had been worked on by several others on the committee and their work was finally agreed after considerable discussion and some amendment.

"There is clear evidence that a determined assault is being made on family life, moral standards and decency in public entertainment and the mass media," it read. "There also seems to be a reluctance in Government departments, the media and even in some church circles to affirm any absolute moral standards." It went on to say that while "filth" had been portrayed in the past it was done surreptiously. "Now it is being shown openly as being 'normal'. We, like many others, are concerned about the environmental pollution of all kinds that is damaging the world today, but in particular we wish: (a) to alert and inform Christians and others like minded to the dangers of moral pollution; (b) to translate into action the concern that hundreds of thousands feel about the moral pollution in our nation today; (c) to register the support of people of goodwill for Christian moral standards in such a way that the national leadership is influenced; (d) to witness to the good news about Jesus Christ."

The Statement went on to give information about the Trafalgar Square and Hyde Park rallies and a list of those on the Council of Reference and the Executive Committee. An appendix was added listing some of the examples of moral pollution in the media which supported the committee's contention. It was a rather slender document bringing together seven or eight examples which were hardly representative of the real situation, but which nevertheless gave some evidence of the committee's concern. Reference was made to the play *Council of Love* and the revue *Oh Calcutta!*; the films *Myra Breckenridge* and *Beyond the Valley of the Dolls*; Dr. Martin Cole's sex education film *Growing up* and the BBC television play *Central Line*. In the field of literature the *Little Red School Book* was cited and reference was made to an article in *The Times* of March 23 by the writer David Holbrook (another of those who had recently returned from a period overseas) in which he drew attention to current trends in literature and music.

During the next few weeks and in the course of its many re-typings the Appendix was amended and altered several times. Some of those who received it objected to the frankness of the details included. The committee itself felt there was a need for more documentation, and during the summer months of 1971 two further developments took place in the media which in one sense played right into the Festival's hands: Ken Russell's film *The Devils* was released; and the *Oz* obscenity trial took place. These two examples were added to the appendix together with comments on some BBC sex education programmes for schools.

There was much discussion at the June 2 committee about the setting of a target figure for attendance on the 25th. Peter Hill had thought in terms of 100,000, others thought 50,000, whilst a few had contemplated a quarter of a million. It was eventually agreed to set a target figure of 100,000. Eddy Stride and Nigel Goodwin were asked to form sub-committees to organize the Trafalgar Square and Hyde Park rallies respectively. Well-known speakers would be booked for the former, which would last from 3 p.m. to 4 p.m. and proclamations to the Government, the media and the Church would be read. The Hyde Park rally would last from 5 p.m. to 10 p.m. It was agreed to hold an inaugural rally at the Westminster Central Hall on a date early in September to arouse interest and support for the events of September 25, and other activities associated with the Festival.

With less than three months to go before the inaugural rally the pressure started to build up during June. Plans were prepared for a leaflet announcing the Festival. Drafts of suitable wording were drawn up by Malcolm Muggeridge and some committee members, and a form of words based on all the suggestions was agreed. The leaflet was carefully worded to avoid giving a negative impression. The phrase which was to be used a great deal in connection with the Festival—"a positive stand for purity, love and family life"—was first used in this leaflet. A young designer, Nick Butterworth, was called in to advise on layout and design. He and Peter Hill discussed the matter into the early hours of one morning before they were satisfied they had the answer. The front cover of the leaflet contained the now familiar outline of the British Isles in white on a dark blue background with light radiating from the island into the surrounding darkness.

Meanwhile at 37 Eastwood Road, the headquarters of the Festival were gradually taking shape. It had been decided to utilize the whole of the ground floor of the house for offices for the Festival and accommodation for Peter and Janet. Kay Stevens was still trying to smarten up the premises following the departure of the MAF staff—a task she never finally completed. Extra furniture, desks, shelves and office equipment were picked up at second hand furniture stores and through advertisements. More names were added to the Council of Reference during June—Dora Bryan the actress, Ernest Shippam, Judge Ruttle, Sir Cyril Black, the Rev. John Caiger a Baptist minister from Gunnersbury, the Rev. John Stott, the Rev. Paul Tucker and the Bishops of Winchester and Willesden. As information about the Festival started to become known several organizations volunteered their support, among them Campus Crusade for Christ, Operation Mobilization and the Church Youth Fellowships Association. New names were added to the Executive Committee: Bernard Madden, a young graphical designer, and Maxwell Creasey, a director of Metropolitan Estates.

During June, Peter Hill was trying to establish a network of regional co-ordinators throughout the country. Their task would be to inform churches in their area about the Festival of Light, arrange rallies and beacon-lightings in provincial centres during September, encourage people in their area to support the Day of Prayer and to attend the national rallies on the 25th (making the travel arrangements if necessary), feed the local press and regional television with information about the Festival and seek ways of maintaining the impact of the Festival after the first phase was over. He had a large number of names and addresses of likely candidates both through his own personal contacts and those of other members of the Executive Committee. Letters were sent to between 500 and 600 people in all, asking them to be a regional co-ordinator or to suggest somebody in their area who could take it on.

The response to the initial request for co-ordinators was slow but as further information was made available about the Festival so the number grew and by the time the final details were being agreed about the Festival's programme the number of regional co-ordinators stood at 130. Peter Hill had a large map of the country on which he marked off the areas covered as the letters came in. The West Country in general and Cornwall and Devon in particular reacted promptly and enthusiastically to the idea and within a few weeks they had made arrangements for a large number of rallies and beacon lightings to take place in their part of the world. East Anglia and several areas in the north were slow to respond, but many of them were covered by the time the Festival programme got under way.

At the Festival headquarters Steve and Kay Stevens were fully occupied in dealing with correspondence, telephone calls and other office work. It was clear that as the Festival gained further momentum they would need additional help. Two young students at the Christian Life College, Poole, offered their services for the summer—Nick Cuthbert and Bob Lloyd. They were to play a vital part in keeping the office routine working satisfactorily, but their first commission was to visit the Keswick Convention during July to publicize the Festival to the thousands who would attend.

By this time the Executive Committee were meeting every week in an effort to keep the stream of ideas and decisions flowing smoothly. Several important decisions were reported to the committee meeting on June 30. The regional co-ordinator for Bristol, Peter Lyne, had agreed to be responsible for the beacon lighting arrangements. A proposal was made that in association with the Festival there should be a Nationwide Day of Prayer on the Sunday preceding the great London rallies. Official approval and the backing of the Churches was to be sought through the Archbishop of Canterbury, Cardinal Heenan, leaders of the Free Churches and the Salvation Army. An *ad hoc* press sub-committee chaired by Paul Cunningham and including journalists, met at the end of June. With the setting up of this sub-committee the Festival organizers took the first step in releasing information about their plans to the world at large. Unfortunately, as they were to find out, the operation was not to be without its problems.

Chapter Two

LET THERE BE LIGHT

It is easy to see in retrospect where the Festival organizers went wrong in their early dealing with the press. For one thing it was expecting perhaps a little too much Christian charity on the part of the press to react enthusiastically to a campaign which as part of its published propaganda slated the media for "giving a tremendous thrust" to such things as "pornography, obscene spectacles and the systematic corruption of the young". It is clear too that the Festival should have been looking for someone who was skilled in public relations, or was at least experienced as a press officer, rather than a journalist, however well-intentioned.

There was one basic misunderstanding from the start. Dan Wooding, a young journalist on the press sub-committee, was a "stringer" for the national press, i.e., in addition to his job as a reporter on his local weekly paper he made it his job to feed "stories", or reports to the Fleet Street dailies and the Press Association concerning his own area or any other events he might hear about. As a result when he agreed to handle the Festival's "launching story" for the national dailies he did so as a freelance journalist on to a good story and not as the Festival's public relations man—a distinction which he claims they never understood though he explained it many times.

Confirmation that Trafalgar Square was booked for September 25 came through on the second week in July (it is not possible to book it more than three months in advance), so he drew up a story based on the information he had received using some quotes from Malcolm Muggeridge. with the headline "Biggest ever demo against porn". It concentrated on the anti-porn aspect. Not until the end of the story was there any mention made of the positive aims of the Festival. Before submitting the story to the national press he 'phoned Steve Stevens to check some facts and verify a few details. Stevens asked for the positive aspect to be strengthened by emphasizing that the Festival was upholding "love and family life", as well as opposing "pornography and moral pollution". Despite the addition of the positive phrase "for love and family life" in the press release, all but two of the papers, *The Times* and the *Daily Telegraph*, emphasized in their head-lines that the demonstration was to be "anti-porn".

That first press announcement contained a small but significant error stating: "The organisers expect more than 100,000 people to attend." In fact the Festival committee had set a *target* of 100,000 which was a very different matter. Once they were on record as *expecting* more than that number they could hardly back-pedal and say it was merely a target.

Nick Cuthbert and Bob Lloyd, the two young student volunteers, arrived at the Keswick Convention mid-way through the first week and immediately started distributing the Festival leaflets, 200,000 of which had been printed in faith that the booking of Trafalgar Square for September 25 would be confirmed. They managed to persuade several car owners to display posters and placards announcing the Festival on their cars which were then parked in strategic positions near the entrance to the huge tents in which the meetings were held. This mass distribution of some ten to fifteen thousand leaflets at Keswick undoubtedly helped to put the Festival on the map as far as many evangelicals were concerned. Many people asked for bulk supplies in order to make copies available to others in their locality. In addition arrangements were made to have the leaflet inserted in the August issues of *Crusade* magazine and *Decision*, the monthly organ of the Billy Graham Evangelistic Association, thereby circulating between 30,000 and 35,000 copies.

When Nick and Bob returned from Keswick they settled into a routine which was to keep them busy for the next few months. Letters were arriving at the rate of up to forty a day seeking information about the Festival and offering support. Little realizing how big the eventual filing system would become they went out and brought a spring clip file (debating whether they would need a second one) in which they kept the incoming letters, answering each one with a typed reply which soon gave way to a duplicated note.

To enable them to spend the maximum amount of time on the job it was decided to provide board and lodging for the two students on the premises. Kay Stevens prepared and furnished an attic room for the two boys, clearing out cupboards and making it as pleasant as she could. Another room on the ground floor had to be decorated. A handyman was engaged to do the ceiling and paper the walls after Kay had done the painting. But she was still the only typist in the office and with all the typing required she fell behind with the painting. She would be on a ladder trying to keep one step ahead of the man who was papering when someone would come and ask for a stencil to be cut. The typing had to come first and some of the painting has been left undone to this day.

The items of office equipment required seemed to be available just when they were needed. They twice borrowed a folding-machine from MAF; they found a small, but useful, guillotine in a second-hand wardrobe they had bought for Peter and Janet's room; and Mr. and Mrs. White of White's Homes (a local orphanage) generously offered their new electric duplicator for the Festival's use. Such was the size of the Festival's duplicating requirements that the Whites hardly made use of it at all during the three months following its arrival. There was a regular shuttle service between the two buildings with young people staggering under the weight of reams of duplicating paper.

White's Homes also provided one of the early helpers, Perrin Firmin, a fifteen year old girl who was about to go to college. Every morning she would come across to the Festival headquarters, sit down and open the mail, pass it to Nick and Bob who decided what should be sent, before giving it back to Perrin to address the envelopes and send out material as requested. Towards the end of July the pressure of secretarial work became such that Kay could no longer cope on her own. This was made a matter of prayer and shortly afterwards two young fully qualified secretaries offered their services, Rosamund Conner, a Roman Catholic who had at one time been Col. Dobbie's secretary and who had been Minutes Secretary at the Festival's Executive Committee meetings since the beginning of June, and Ruth Mason, who contacted the Festival office to see if they needed help after a friend had shown her a copy of the Festival leaflet.

During July the work of the Executive Committee was somewhat hampered by the claim of holidays, but progress was being made along all fronts. Judy Mackenzie, an increasingly well-known gospel folk singer who composes most of her own material, offered to write a special song for the Festival. Somewhat non-committal but friendly letters were received from Cardinal Heenan and the Archbishop of Canterbury in reply to the information sent to them regarding the Nationwide Day of Prayer. The committee felt that much more publicity needed to be given to this aspect of the Festival. Prayer support was increasing all the time and by the middle of July the mailing list has risen to around 500 names, to each of whom a copy of the prayer letter was sent.

There was by now a growing feeling on the Executive Committee that an experienced press officer was a vital necessity with all the complex press and public relations arrangements that needed to be made in time for the Festival's main events. One of the committee members, Jack Wallace, a London solicitor and a leading evangelical layman in the Church of England, suggested the name of Peter Thompson, one of his clients, and, as it happened, his secretary's newly-acquired husband. Thompson was an experienced public relations man having been involved in the late 1950's and early 1960's with a vigorous campaign for penal reform in association with Lord Longford. He had spent sometime himself in Broadmoor with mental illness, but was now public relations officer with the National Council of YMCA's in London and had recently taken his own one-man action to combat sex in the cinema. At the end of May he went to a cinema in Hammersmith with his two children by a previous marriage to see the Walt Disney film *101 Dalmations*. During the programme a U certificate trailer for an X certificate film *Soldier Blue* was shown including a scene where a Red Indian woman was stripped, raped and mutilated. Children in the audience were crying and screaming and he rushed out to see the manager to get him to take the trailer off. Though he was unsuccessful at the time, as a result of his representations the trailer was subsequently withdrawn from London cinemas.

Meanwhile the committee had another major problem on its hands. Col. Dobbie met senior police officers at Cannon Row Police Station on July 28 together with representatives of the Festival. They were told that Trafalgar Square was filled to capacity with 25,000 people, although another 25,000 could be accommodated in the surrounding area blocking all roads round the square and stretching down to the Embankment. In view of this the police suggested that the whole Festival be held in Hyde Park.

But there were difficulties at the Park also. When approached, the Department of The Environment was, in Col. Dobbie's words "neutral about the whole Festival" (use of the Park was normally restricted to officially sponsored events). But though the speeches could be amplified there was a rule in all the Royal Parks that music could not (even transistor radios were banned). When the American evangelist Billy Graham had spoken at a rally in Hyde Park during the mid-sixties his soloist, Beverley Shea, had had to sing without a microphone. The committee discussed the confused situation at length but despite the difficulties, felt that they ought to go ahead as planned both in Trafalgar

Square and Hyde Park. Their application went in and they awaited the haggling. There was no haggling. Everything they asked for was granted. Subsequently they agreed to curtail the Hyde Park rally following representations made to them by the Police and Park authorities. It was re-timed to start at 4 p.m. and finish at 7.30 p.m.

By the end of July the Council of Reference was all but complete. The new names included Dr. G. R. Beasley Murray, principal of Spurgeon's College, London, the Bishop of Blackburn, Tom Chapman, the broadcaster, Dr. Ernest Claxton, formerly Secretary of the British Medical Association, Sir Maurice Parsons, formerly deputy governor of the Bank of England, David Kossoff, the actor, and John Boyd, the trades unionist. The four remaining names were added in August – Lord Beswick, Chief Labour Whip in the House of Lords, Lord Stamford, Mrs. Peggy Fenner, Conservative MP for Chatham, and Ron Lewis, Labour MP for Carlisle.

At the Festival headquarters at South Woodford a notable landmark was passed in early August, when for the first time a hundred letters were received in the morning post. Numbers had been gradually increasing towards the end of July and from the middle of August onwards they averaged between eighty to a hundred a day. The atmosphere on the ground floor of 37 Eastwood Road had to be experienced to be believed. It was the summer holidays and a seemingly endless stream of young people turned up to give a hand, counting leaflets, folding posters, filling envelopes, stamping them and taking them over to the post office in the huge sacks provided. Publicity material for the Festival had been building up steadily since the first leaflets were produced. 10,000 posters using the same idea of a radiant Britain shining in the darkness had been printed, together with a large number of car stickers with the slogan "Moral pollution needs a solution". By this time too a large amount of duplicated material concerning the Festival had been produced, including the Statement of Intent and Appendix, the "Prayer and Progress" letters and details concerning regional co-ordinators.

The basic pattern of earlier weeks was still followed, incoming mail being opened and dealt with during the morning, filing, packing, duplicating in the afternoon; but as the Festival became more widely known there was an additional hazard—the telephone which most days scarcely stopped ringing from eight o'clock in the morning to eleven o'clock at night. On occasions it rang as soon as the receiver was replaced, such was the pressure of incoming calls. Nick Cuthbert's fiancée, a nurse, had such difficulty getting through to the office on the 'phone that she made an arrangement with some of her friends. Whenever any of them passed the 'phone, which was at the bottom of the stairs in the nurses home they would dial the Festival number and if by chance they managed to get through—a rare occurrence—they shouted for Lois to come to the 'phone!

It was obvious that many people who tried to 'phone the Festival office were just giving up in despair. They applied for a second telephone little expecting to find the G.P.O. on the doorstep within two days. ("A miracle" said Col. Dobbie who had recently had to wait nine months for a similar installation at his office!) So as to save wasting the time of those busy packing, typing and so on, the telephone was put out in the passage. A cousin of Col. Dobbie's, Honor Cottingham, volunteered as telephonist, and the sound of her cultured voice answering the 'phone with "Festival of Light, can I help you? . . . Oh, you want despatch", conjuring up visions of a well-ordered commercial enterprise, reduced members of the staff to helpless laughter at times. Humour was a natural safety valve when they were under so much pressure, and there was a great deal of high-spirited fun.

Press reporters and photographers were regular visitors, marvelling at the number of young people swarming around the house.

In order to use the time to the fullest extent some days there were three sittings for lunch, saving the time many of the young people would have spent getting home and back to eat. At evening meals there were seldom less than eight to cook for, and there were always odd snacks for those not around at meal times. The problems did not stop there however. Some nights all the beds in the house were occupied by visitors of one sort or another and quite often Steve and Kay and other members of the family had to sleep on the floor, which may have accounted for the fact that on several occasions they did not go to bed (or floor) until one o'clock in the morning, to be up again at 6 a.m. to carry on with the work.

Steve and Peter, of course, not only had responsibility for the work done at headquarters; they were also involved in the numerous Executive and sub-committee meetings, most of which went on late into the night. One such was the first meeting of the public relations sub-committee which Peter Thompson had been asked to set up. The meeting, which took place at Thompson's Earls Court flat, was attended by Mary Whitehouse and went on until half past eleven that night. For three hours after they had gone, Thompson hammered out the first ever co-ordinated public relations policy for the Festival. A comprehensive list of over four hundred names and addresses was drawn up comprising newspapers, press agencies, and individuals in responsible positions in the press and broadcasting, to which all the subsequent major press releases about the Festival were sent. A programme of press conferences and press releases was prepared, with the aim of capitalizing on incidents and issues as they occurred, to notify the press and gain publicity for the Festival, i.e., when Lord Longford withdrew from the Council of Reference because of his involvement with his own Commission on Pornography, or when Cardinal Heenan, leader of the British Roman Catholic Church, agreed to his commendation of the Festival being made public.

The Executive Committee, meeting on August 10, gave the go-ahead to Thompson's PR policy, and also heard reports on various other aspects of the Festival's plans. Operation Beacon, as the beacon-lighting had come to be known, was attracting enthusiastic support and confirmation had been received concerning the lighting of at least forty beacons. Among ideas forthcoming in connection with the beacon-lighting were suggestions for the ringing of church bells, torchlight processions, candles burning in windows, barbeques, garden bonfires, electric beacons on tops of churches and buildings, a ring of floodlights and even an illuminated barge on the Thames.

One of the issues which was being raised with increasing urgency by some members of the committee was the question of what should happen after the Festival. Eddy Stride had first raised it in mid-July when it was agreed that a follow-up committee should be formed and directives prepared. This appears to have been one suggestion which was not taken up and was subsequently to lead to several problems after the London rallies were over and people were looking for guidance and leadership as to the next step.

By this time Peter Hill had travelled many hundreds of miles taking meetings about the Festival. A series in the West Country, in Exeter, Plymouth, Yeovil, Redruth and Taunton was followed by visits to the Midlands and Cambridge and Oxford. Everywhere he went there was enthusiastic support for the Festival. People kept coming up to him and saying, "We've been praying for something like this for years". In places where plans for the Festival were already quite well-known he found a great many people who were praying regularly and specifically for every aspect of the Festival's activities. It was this nationwide prayer support, he is convinced, which in the end won the day.

On August 25, with one month to go before the London rallies and less than a fortnight before the inaugural rally at Westminster Central Hall, the organization moved into top gear. Over 2,500 tickets had been requested for the Central Hall meeting, the Festival leaflets were going out in quantities averaging 5,000 a day, making a total at that time of around a quarter of a million leaflets in circulation, 7,000 posters had been sent out and another 10,000 were on order. To add to the storage and distribution problems a further item of publicity material was added to those already available. Arthur Wallis had telephoned from Devon earlier in the month to suggest the production of lapel badges similar to those used on flag days. Steve Stevens came up with the idea of a design incorporating beacon flames and this was brilliantly interpreted by Nick Butterworth. (The design was so successful that it subsequently became the symbol of the Festival.) 300,000 badges were delivered to the office together with fifty six pounds of metal pins. Someone was immediately despatched upstairs to weigh the pins into hundreds so that the right number could go out with the badges.

It was at this point that Steve Stevens decided a mailing should be undertaken to the 2,000 or so names on the mailing list. "It can't be done", was the plaintive cry of his overworked staff, but it was. The envelopes were addressed from the files within three or four days entirely by voluntary help —women's groups in the South Woodford area and any one of the dozens of young people who dropped in to the headquarters for a few hours. All available personnel were crammed into the office to speed the collating, folding and inserting of material into the envelopes.

Ten sample badges were dispatched with a progress report to every address on the mailing list. The progress report sent out in the mailing gave encouraging news of activities planned in Devon and Cornwall, Buckinghamshire, Hampshire, Essex, Dorset, Sussex, Monmouthshire, Derbyshire and the areas around Bristol, Swindon, Barnstaple and Cardiff. In addition a leaflet giving prayer topics for use on the Nationwide Day of Prayer and an article on Biblical Morality prepared by the Rev. Paul Tucker were included in the mailing.

Amidst all the hectic day-to-day activity at the Festival headquarters, plans were quietly being laid for the inaugural meeting at Westminster Central Hall. Maxwell Creasey was the Executive Committee member responsible for making these arrangements. By the end of August the list of speakers was more or less complete and the general outline of the programme was agreed. The two main speakers were to be Malcolm Muggeridge and the Bishop of Stepney, the Rt. Rev. Trevor Huddleston. The former was, of course, no surprise, but the latter's name associated with the Festival caused several raised eyebrows. A humanitarian and a liberal-minded man, he was best known for his opposition to racial prejudice, particularly in southern Africa and since his arrival in this country two years previously he had been an outspoken advocate of racial harmony in his East London sub-diocese. He had not publicly taken a stand on the specific issues of obscenity and pornography until he gave his support to a protest organized by Eddy Stride and Paul Tucker, over a sex film on general release at a cinema in East London, earlier in the year.

In two interviews published around this time he made clear his reasons for supporting the Festival. "If you are going to preach the Christian gospel, you have got to say something about chastity. It is integral to the gospel and bunk to say that it isn't. That doesn't mean you are attacking homosexuals. It doesn't mean you are a rabid censorship maniac. I'm not any of those things—they go very much against the grain indeed. The sort of assumption that people are making is that because I don't think it is a good idea to show a dirty film to a child in Stepney then I must mean that it is a good idea for a child to die of hunger in Bengal. There is absurdity in that logic.

"I am going to let my voice be heard against unchastity because I am a Christian, not because I am against freedom. I have taken a vow of chastity and I would deny my own vocation if I did not do it. I should have thought I had done enough in my life to show that I care deeply about freedom. Pornography is something that is introduced by a decadent, bored people and it creates an obsession which is dangerous. It is twisting the true meaning of sexuality and therefore of human life; twisting it into something which is totally trivial. It puts the meaning of love on to such an incredibly shallow plane that the whole of our thinking is going to be mucked up by it. But I don't want to exaggerate. I still think it is an infinitely worse thing to let people die of malnutrition."

The supporting speakers were to be Mrs. Joan Carroll Gibbons, widow of the famous dance band leader, Johannes Facius, co-author of the Danish *Little White Book* (an answer to the *Little Red School Book*), the Rev. Alan Caple, minister of an Elim Pentecostal Church in Birmingham, and Mrs. Jean Rees, widow of the well-known evangelist from Hildenborough Hall. In addition Lonnie Frisbee, one of the Children of God Jesus People, Cliff Richard and Ted Lyons, from the Mayflower Family Centre in Canning Town, were to speak about their Christian faith.

In view of the demand for tickets for the meeting it was agreed to arrange an overflow meeting with closed-circuit television in the lecture hall and library below which could seat another 1,100, bringing the total number of seats available to 3,700. When the idea of using closed-circuit TV was first put forward the high cost (£500) was something of a deterrent. However not only was £350 donated directly towards meeting this cost, but large screen projection (normally costing another £500) in place of monitor sets was also included with no extra charge. Previous experience with similar meetings suggested that twenty per cent of the free ticket allocation could be double-booked to take account of tickets originally issued and not being taken up. To cope with any disruptive tactics or opposition within the hall a strong body of marshals was recruited. It could hardly have been visualized how necessary they were going to be.

During the latter part of August Peter Thompson's public relations campaign swung into operation. He had inherited what the media saw as virtually a Whitehouse/Muggeridge anti-porn crusade. He was anxious to introduce to the media the young people involved in the Festival and emphasize its positive aspects rather than its negative attitudes. The numerous personal contacts he had in press, radio and television were diligently followed up after the initial information was sent to them in August. In all, Thompson reckons he made as many as 1,500 telephone calls during the run-up period to the London rallies, and was in receipt of sometimes as many as thirty calls a day from people in the world of press and broadcasting. Through this constant contact and the feeding of information and ideas for coverage, the media gradually took notice of the existence of the Festival as a significant event and started to make arrangements to cover its plans and development.

At the same time as all this was taking place he had inaugurated his own campaign to get the Ken Russell film *The*

Devils off the London screens. He had been to see the film shortly after it was released in London and was very concerned about its mixture of sadism, sex and violence. From previous experience he was well aware of the social casualties that could result from exposure to such a film and he began extensive lobbying of the members of the Public Services Committee of the Greater London Council who had the power to revoke the licence granted to the film. As it turned out he failed by three votes to secure its rejection, but in subsequent months the film was banned in Glasgow and Blackpool.

Letters coming into the Festival headquarters at South Woodford virtually doubled during the first few days in September. The previous week's mailing, the further distribution of leaflets and large advertisements in the Christian press obviously had an effect, together with the return of many people from their holidays, and on September 2 no less than 233 letters dropped on to the front door mat of 37 Eastwood Road. By the beginning of the week of the inaugural rally some 400,000 leaflets had been despatched, together with innumerable car stickers, sheets of beacon badges and posters. The beacon design, greatly enlarged, was to feature on a new batch of posters expected from the printer in time for the September 9 rally, for which nearly 5,000 applications for tickets had been received.

As it turned out 300 of those tickets had been requested by members of what was to become loosely termed "the opposition". They had, of course, been able to seek information about the Festival just as easily as those interested in it for positive reasons. Early in September the B.B.C. contacted Peter Thompson with a tip-off, later confirmed by the Police, that there would be some sort of invasion by a group representing various members of underground movements who would seek to disrupt the inaugural meeting and cause trouble. Many opponents of the Festival felt that in deciding to openly oppose it in this way the underground movements concerned were making a tactical error. They were crediting the Festival with a greater significance than most people in the media were prepared to accord it, and were giving additional publicity to an event which but for their protest might have gone virtually unnoticed. That the inaugural rally made front page news on the following day in many of the nation's newspapers was in no small part due to the efforts of the underground movements which so actively opposed it.

Chapter Three

SWITCHING ON THE LIGHT

"Bogus nuns disrupt anti-porn rally." Whatever other headlines the Festival of Light organizers had hoped might result from the inaugural rally in Westminster Central Hall on September 9, that was hardly one which they could have expected. How such a headline came to appear in the nation's newspapers the following morning is told in some detail in a later chapter. Suffice it to say here that it could not be attributed to the Festival's press conference held in Fleet Street on Thursday morning—at least only in a very indirect way.

Peter Hill spoke first, explaining how he had received a vision after returning from India and how, following its confirmation, he had sought the assistance of those who shared his concern. Considering it was his first ever press conference he did not do at all badly, though it was unwise of him to chase one red herring drawn across his path by a lady journalist about whether or not he would like to see a naked woman walking down the street. Col. Dobbie emphasized that the Festival was more than just an attempt to stem the spread of pornography, it was meant to have positive results—to promote love, purity and family life. The organizers of the Festival of Light were opposed to all forms of moral pollution, he said, violence, pornography and even the pollution of the English language. Plans were outlined for the beacon-lightings and the rallies at Trafalgar

Square and Hyde Park and someone rather unwisely suggested that there might be as many as a quarter of a million people taking part. (This appears to have been the only time when anyone representing the Festival officially estimated a figure as large as this. It was subsequently taken up by *The Times*, the London *Evening News* and the *Church Times*, and for some reason doubled by the *Salisbury Journal*, as an estimate of the number expected.)

One of the reporters asked if the Festival had the backing of Church leaders and in the course of his reply Col. Dobbie said that the Archbishop of Canterbury had declined to give the Festival his support. At this, John Miles, the Archbishop's press officer jumped up to contest Col. Dobbie's statement. He said that Dr. Ramsey had sent a letter to the organizers in July in which he said that he shared their concern about the over-concentration of nudity and sex in the entertainment industry and would continue to pray about the matter. Miles said that this letter was the "most appropriate kind of support". In answer to later questions Col. Dobbie stated that he had written to the Archbishop to suggest that churches might make Sunday, September 19, a Nationwide Day of Prayer for the reinstatement of moral standards, and that Dr. Ramsey had written back saying that he would be unable to do so because it was Ordination Sunday.

"I rang him up particularly and asked if he could give us formal blessing," said Col. Dobbie. "He did not."

These two references to the Archbishop were dealt with by Dobbie in matter-of-fact terms. The reactions of the pressmen present revealed that they had read more significance into his words than he intended. As will be seen, some of them proceeded to make a meal out of a small crumb.

Malcolm Muggeridge waxed eloquent in his customary style. "When society has no sense of moral order it finds it has no sense of order whatsoever," he said, and went on to enlarge on what he called "carnal eroticism and sexual attraction". He quoted from Romans 8: 6, "For to be carnally minded is death but to be spiritually minded is life and peace". But, asked a reporter, didn't all this emphasis on corruption suggest that it was more a Festival of Darkness than a Festival of Light? Muggeridge disagreed. It was a wrong impression, he said. "There is an infinitely happier, more beautiful, more loving way of living. What we want to show on September 25 is that this light shines more brightly than ever." Was not spreading salvation and enlightenment more radical than just making rules, he was asked. Was not the cart before the horse? "There must be a level of practicality," he replied. "None of us would agree that there is any kind of absolute in it." It was terrible for example, that people had to earn their living by publicly degrading their bodies. While the Festival of Light might bring some illumination into ordinary lives, he felt sadly that there was no salvation however for the mass media. "I can see the media might be a little less terrible," he said, "but I don't expect to turn on the television set with any great feeling of uplift."

Bishop Trevor Huddleston told the assembled press-men that pornography was "an assault on human dignity". Anything which assaulted man was in fact blasphemous. "I would like the Church to be unafraid of saying that chastity is part of the gospel. Advocating a stricter view of morality does not mean that we lack compassion—we understand people's frailties."

One of the two Danes at the conference Johnny Noer, was given an opportunity to speak. A statement had been issued to the press which gave their interpretation of events in Denmark since the lifting of all restrictions on the sale of pornographic material, together with a philosophical background detailing the events that led up to this decision on the part of the Danish Government. Their first concern was to expose the fallacy in the supposed decrease in sex crimes in Denmark since pornography had been freely available. They pointed out that two years before that happened, legislation in Denmark had been changed with regard to homosexual prostitution, incest between father and daughter and other close relatives, immorality towards children, rape, and the age below which seduction was punishable. In addition there had been a falling tendency to record sexual crimes, thus suggesting that it was not the sex crimes which had decreased but the reporting of those crimes, and the fact that what were formerly crimes had now become exempt. What had risen beyond any doubt was the incidence of gonorrhoea which had increased from its 1966 figure of 7,162 cases to 31,172 cases in 1969. Johnny Noer said that in Denmark pornography was becoming increasingly "brutal and sadistic". "We warn the British people against joining us on the same road to shame," he concluded.

And that—apart from a few contributions from one or two Festival personnel in the wings—was that.

As it transpired the events of the press conference were rather over-shadowed by the subsequent developments at the inaugural rally, but very few of the papers carried anything very positive about the real aims and intentions of the Festival. Both the BBC and independent television channels carried reports of the Festival on their news bulletins, and during the early evening period Malcolm Muggeridge and Cliff Richard did battle with John Mortimer QC and Charlotte Rampling on BBC's "Nationwide" programme while Peter Hill faced the cameras alone on Thames Television's "Today" programme.

Apart from attending the morning press conference everybody from the Festival headquarters spent most of the day at the Westminster Central Hall getting the premises ready for the evening meeting. The huge arc-lights were installed for the Canadian television cameras which were filming the meeting and also for the closed circuit TV cameras feeding pictures to the overflow meeting below. A large white banner proclaiming "Nationwide Festival of Light" was strung across the hall in front of the magnificent organ.

Well before the advertised hour the crowds gathered for the start of the meeting. The services of the London Emmanuel Choir had been secured to assist with the singing and they filed into the hall at 6.30 to give half an hour's preliminary music. They brought a touch of colour and formality to the proceedings with their smart red capes and immaculate evening dress. At seven o'clock Col. Dobbie came to the microphone as the platform party filed in and introduced Nigel Goodwin as the compére for the evening. Together with all the speakers, he had been briefed on the likelihood of some disturbance during the meeting. Stewards had noticed several members of the audience who, to say the least, looked unlikely to be supporters of the Festival. Among the characters regarded with suspicion were half a dozen "nuns". Stewards quickly spotted that some of them were young men in disguise. To minimize trouble a steward was stationed behind each of the "nuns" in the audience!

After a few preliminary remarks Nigel Goodwin introduced the audience to Peter Hill. Once more he outlined his vision of the Festival and stressed the importance in local follow-ups to the Festival after its climax on September 25. He was followed by Steve Stevens who made some routine announcements and Peter Lyne who carefully explained the purpose of the beacons to be lit on September 23. Nigel Goodwin came to the microphone again. "I hope you're getting some good vibes," he said, not perhaps realizing how close those vibes were.

Bishop Trevor Huddleston was the first main speaker. Gaunt, precise and with obvious sincerity he delivered his address.

"I believe that part of the sickness of today" he said, "is that we are deluged with words through the mass media to such an extent that we find it almost impossible to distinguish truth from falsehood.

"I stand here because I believe that there is only one gospel and at the very heart of it there is a view or vision of human life which is valid for the whole man."

He explained that holiness and wholeness were one and the same and that within the holiness to which men were called there was a place for chastity and purity of heart. Not to strive for purity of heart was to miss out on the meaning of life.

He then developed the theme of the dignity of man which he held Christians believed as no others could, because of their belief that God not only made man in His image but became man in Christ. Anything that offended human dignity was not only obscene but also blasphemous.

"For me" he said, "the definition of pornography or obscenity is very simple. It is the abuse of that which is made in the image and likeness of God for any end whatsoever". By such a definition racism and the countless examples of man's inhumanity to man were obscene but by the same token the Christian was bound to proclaim his belief in the moral law because it existed to protect man's dignity.

He noted certain assumptions that made his position difficult to proclaim in the present generation. It was widely assumed that to profess chastity as a virtue was to be guilty of deceit. It was frequently assumed that to care about one aspect of morality implied a lack of concern about other equally important areas. He rejected these opinions as "totally and absolutely false".

A third problem that inhibited positive Christian witness to chastity was the crisis of faith in the Church as it faced times of bewildering change involving a host of new ethical challenges.

He concluded as he had begun with an unabashed proclamation of purity of heart as a "fully positive" concept carrying "within itself the very meaning of life".

"And if that is not important—if this is not a moral issue then I don't know what is. I cannot conceive that it is in any man to fight against racism; to fight against the evils of war; to fight against all the inhumanities which man commits against man unless we proclaim the end for which man is created—which is the glory of God!"

The audience erupted into applause—as it had done at points during the address. The objectors who had revealed themselves during the address by occasional bursts of ill-timed clapping had nevertheless given Huddleston a hearing. This may have been due to his impressive presence and forceful diction. It may have been that they were holding their fire. Many in the crowd began to sense that a conflict was taking place.

Judy Mackenzie, the young gospel folk singer, was next at the microphone with her own composition "Let there be light", the song she wrote especially for the Festival.

"Yesterday's dream didn't quite come true,
We fought for our freedom—and what did it do?
Laughed out the old laws, and brought in the new.
Now no-one can see where we stand.

Let there be light in the land,
Let there be light in the people,
Let there be God in our lives from now on.

So many people are waiting to find
Peace for the body and peace for the mind.
While there is darkness, the spirit is blind,
But when there is God there is sight."

As she finished singing it a voice from the gallery shouted, "That's prostitution of music". Others shouted abuse but the outbreak soon subsided.

Joan Gibbons then came forward to give her testimony. She began confidently, forcefully and humorously, evoking bursts of laughter from the crowd. Then suddenly a girl's voice pierced the hall and stopped the speaker: "We reject that morality—death to the family!" Joan Gibbons was forced to stop but if she had been shaken by the outburst it didn't show. She waited her moment and then came back with, "O.K. boys—I used to be like that when I was young years ago!" A supportive burst of applause broke from the Christians present.

"What you need" she said firmly and almost maternally, "is the power of the Holy Spirit of God!" At this there was more applause and Joan Gibbons, perhaps patronizingly but certainly with great directness told her opponents of their need for the Christ she had found.

Johannus Facius of Denmark rose to speak in an atmosphere that was shot with tension and excitement. He said that before travelling to England God had given him a word from the prophet Isaiah (chapter 59: 19): "When the enemy shall come in like a flood, the spirit of the Lord shall lift up a standard against him."

In view of what was being acted out under the dome of the Central Hall, there could hardly have been a more appropriate or encouraging verse.

Facius set out to apply his text to the situation in Denmark concerning the flood of pornographic productions, but the heckling began. Protestors shouted back that starving Bengali children was pornography, war was pornography, Viet Nam was pornography. . . .

Facius tried to complete his address but the opposition was making his task impossible. He stood quietly at the microphone waiting for a chance to continue until a robust young voice called out from another corner of the hall: "We're with you, brother!"

But Facius could make little further progress and before the meeting could disintegrate any further, Muriel Shepherd, conductor of the London Emmanuel Choir, strode to the rostrum and led choir and audience in a warrior-like rendition of the hymn "How Great Thou Art" which more than drowned the protestors' chants.

Nigel Goodwin then called on Malcolm Muggeridge who stepped forward to a mixture of welcoming applause and a resumption of cat-calls. A small man when seen away from the familiar format of the television screen, he appeared strangely vulnerable. Nevertheless he began with his usual panâche, conducting a dialogue with his young opponents, inviting one of them to say his piece and then listen to his own.

Someone called him a "shackled Toby trotted out for special occasions for the benefit of all these people to spew your obscenities . . . ".

At this point there were roars and counter-roars and the mood of the meeting began to take an unpleasant turn. Muggeridge began to appear as unable to hold his own. The choir sang again—a setting of "How sweet the name of Jesus sounds" but even though the stewards were escorting many demonstrators from the hall (working to a careful and firmly courteous code), it was obvious that the battle would recommence after the last verse. It became clear to many of the supporters that it was profoundly important that

Muggeridge should be able to finish his address. To silence a quiet-spoken Dane was one thing, but to stop the meeting's most celebrated speaker could only be seen as a defeat for the platform.

With the hymn concluded, Muggeridge started again. By this time he was making little attempt to follow the carefully prepared speech released at the morning press conference. He tried to speak about the power of the media with their primary concerns to reach as many people as possible, to sell as many things as possible and to stimulate as much consumption as possible. The interruptions continued. "I've been saved!" shouted one mocking demonstrator repeatedly.

Muggeridge paused and said sadly, "I think it's a waste of time to try and develop any sort of cogent thought in the presence of these scattered yahoos". Nevertheless he pressed on pointing out the great difficulty in countering the pollution of words. To take a word like "love" and give it only an erotic connotation would "deprive the language . . . of one of the most beautiful concepts that it contains".

The shouting started up again, the much publicized "nuns" attempted to invade the platform, and Nigel Goodwin intervened pleading for quiet and saying that the speakers were willing to talk with their opponents after the meeting. His plea was ignored.

Muggeridge, now sounding somewhat hoarse, resumed and suggested that the behaviour of the hecklers was a splendid demonstration of "the desperate need" that could only be answered by the message St. Paul had taken to a pagan world, showing very similar characteristics to our present society. "He told them about the Light that comes into the world.

"That Light is the Light that still shines!" exclaimed Muggeridge now obviously deeply moved. "And the purpose of the Festival is that every single person who cares for that Light should shine it in his face, shine it in his words, shine it in his song, shine it in his life so that the relatively few people who are responsible for this moral breakdown of our society will know that they are pitted against, not just a few reactionary people, but all the people in this country who still love this Light—the Light of the world!"

The hall was silent at last as Muggeridge closed with the words of scripture. "The night is far spent, the day is at hand: let us put aside the deeds of darkness. Let us put on the armour of light . . . If God is for us who can be against us?" He sat down amid sustained applause and cheering. He had more than managed to finish his talk. Something of a triumph had taken place.

There were other speakers to come: Cliff Richard, Lonnie Frisbee, Ted Lyons, Jean Rees the evangelist's widow, and the Rev. Alan Caple but they were heard in comparative peace and quiet. The battle, it seemed, was over. Afterwards many prolonged discussions took place between the supporters and opponents of the Festival. Even during the course of the meeting while people were being escorted out, Sister Doreen Gemmel (famed for her Church Army work amongst alcoholic women) had slipped away from her seat to talk with the demonstrators outside and listen to them.

There were differing reports of the number of people who had taken part in the demonstration, ranging from sixty to two hundred. Subsequent newspaper stories confirmed what many at the meeting felt to be true, namely that the opposition was well-planned. It was apparently sponsored by the Gay Liberation Front (a group which seeks to promote complete freedom for homosexuals) together with the Women's Liberation Movement, sympathizers of the underground press and members of street theatres and freedom movements all co-ordinated to form an "anti-repression" movement with the code name Operation Rupert. Each protester at the Central Hall was part of a chronological sequence of demonstrations conducted from the front by a photographer who continually barracked the speakers and signalled to the demonstrators when their turn was due.

Yet in a very real sense the opposition had "made" the meeting. They not only ensured good press coverage, they dramatized the conflict that the Festival of Light was all about.

The *Methodist Recorder* criticized the event "in all

charity" for being little more than a "testimony meeting" when it was billed as something which was to speak for the public conscience. Against this, however, can be set Steve Stevens' own report printed in the *Baptist Times*, *Life of Faith*, and *Catholic Herald*. He closed with the words, "The note of victory had been sounded and one began to feel that this was no longer a sleeping apathetic Church, but the Church triumphant!" His words could have been echoed by anybody in the platform party that evening. As they filed off after the meeting several of them had been visibly moved. "We felt that we had been engaged in a struggle of Light against darkness", said Colonel Dobbie afterwards. "And the Light won!"

Chapter Four

STRIKING A LIGHT

THE FOCUS of attention now switched from London to the provinces. Two men had been chiefly responsible for rallying support around the country, Peter Hill, whose task it was to secure the services of regional co-ordinators in strategic centres, and Peter Lyne, originally the Bristol regional co-ordinator who subsequently undertook to organize Operation Beacon, the mass beacon-lighting which took place on the Thursday before the Festival rallies in London. In both cases a great deal of preparatory work was done by these two, often in collaboration with each other. Letters were sent to contacts in different parts of the country encouraging individuals to seek the support of local churches to arrange some form of localized activity that would draw attention to the Nationwide Festival. By the time the second week in September arrived the number of regional co-ordinators had risen to around 130, and the total number of prospective beacon lightings was between 250 and 300.

There were more than seventy regional rallies around the country during September, with speakers from the Executive Committee and the Council of Reference. The first took place at Weston-Super-Mare, where Eddy Stride was the speaker and the audience no more than a hundred or so. The following day he was joined by Paul Tucker at a rally in Bristol Cathedral. Here it was a different story. The cathedral was packed to capacity with between 600 and 700 people present. One reason for the enthusiastic response to the Festival in the Bristol area was that there had been a demonstration against pornography earlier in the year, when over 500 people joined a march of witness protesting at the opening of a "sex supermarket" in the city.

The third rally in the Bristol area took place on September 6 at Bath Abbey when despite the fact that very little publicity was given to the meeting until the last couple of days, the abbey was full by the time the meeting started, with about 700 people present. At some of the meetings opposition groups appeared. As at the Central Hall event their purposes seemed purely destructive and irrational. The North Somerset Anarchists and members of the Bath Arts Workshop banded together to organize their own style of protest. As people arrived for the meeting a man dressed as a bishop pranced around outside the abbey swinging mock incense and uttering incantations. During the meeting which was constantly heckled, a Hitler-like figure complete with Nazi uniform and small moustache marched into the building and stood underneath the pulpit while Paul Tucker was preaching. He left the abbey together with the other demonstrators during a time of prayer which followed the address giving Nazi salutes and shouting "Death to God" and "Death to the Church". If the counter-demonstration did nothing else, it certainly opened the eyes of those present to a previously unsuspected facet of society as well as providing useful publicity for the Festival. The following evening's newspaper carried a front page story headlined, "Bath Abbey demo by anarchists".

There was trouble, too, at the Ashton Hall, Lancaster, on September 18 at a Festival rally. The police were called on two occasions, first because of intensive heckling by students and, of all people, a city councillor during the main address given by the Bishop of Lancaster, and secondly because of a report that a bomb had been placed underneath the platform. Fortunately the bomb scare turned out to be a hoax. Two days earlier Colonel Dobbie had been in Truro Cathedral to speak at a rally which helped to strengthen the already large support for the Festival in Cornwall. Amongst other rallies during the first half of the month were those at Bournemouth, Cardiff, Plymouth, Manchester, Coventry, Oxford, Blackpool, Reading, York and Nottingham. In Exeter Cathedral, on the same night as the inaugural rally in London, a thousand people gathered to hear Eddy Stride and Johnny Noer, one of the Danish visitors, speak about the threat of pornography.

A letter from the leader of the Liberal Party, Mr. Jeremy Thorpe, was read to the rally in Barnstaple where 700 people were present, in which he said, "I know from correspondence with constituents how many have been distressed by receiving offensive literature through the post. In one case which I referred to the Attorney General the recipient was a girl of nine. I should personally be opposed to any rigid form of censorship but I am convinced that the present law is totally inadequate to protect people, young and old alike, from being deluged through the post, and alas all too often on television, with material that is pornographic and thoroughly offensive to them."

At St. Paul's Church, Winchester, over a thousand people gathered to hear Nigel Goodwin speak about the Festival and subsequently lead a torch-light march from the church to the King Alfred Statue in the centre of the city. Members of the Southampton World Poverty Action Group were present at the meeting and distributed leaflets claiming that the real sins of the world were poverty, racialism, intolerance and war, not the present "slight over-emphasis on sexuality". The leaflet questioned whether those attending the rally had their priorities right and asked if they were indulging in a Festival of Flight rather than a Festival of Light. Nigel Goodwin accepted the challenge and replied to them directly pointing to the remarkable record of the Festival leaders in a wide field of social and humanitarian enterprises.

Not all the rallies were large meetings with big-name speakers. Many were small, semi-private functions, simply designed to inform and enthuse local Christians. Very few of them hit the headlines, except where there was opposition or a disturbance, but they were undoubtedly influential in creating interest in the areas, mobilizing prayer support and stimulating support for the beacon lightings which were to take place two days before the London rallies.

The Nationwide Day of Prayer was observed on Sunday, September 19. It is difficult to assess the significance of this event as there have been very few reports directly relating to it. It never received the sort of national significance or support which was originally hoped for but it is known that in several areas local groups of churches took specific action to spend time during the day in prayer for the nation. At the East London Tabernacle, where the Rev. Paul Tucker is minister, for instance, many members of the church observed the day as one of prayer and fasting. From ten o'clock in the morning until after nine o'clock at night there were several periods of unbroken intercession throughout the day. No less than 400 people were involved at various times during the day and prayer was offered not only for the specific witness of the Festival of Light but also for the spiritual needs of the nation.

Among those who regularly prayed for the Festival were the "Intercessors for Britain", a group comprising more than 1,000 people who covenant to pray one hour every week for Britain. The two leaders of the group, Arthur Wallis and Denis Clark, were both closely associated with Peter Hill when the Festival was no more than a vision and they notified the Intercessors at an early stage, thus ensuring continuous prayer support for it from those who belonged to the group. Wallis later organized a non-stop prayer session during the Hyde Park meeting.

As the night for Operation Beacon drew nearer last minute instructions were sent to the organizers from Peter

Lyne in Bristol. Many of the beacons were to be in the nature of bonfires, and large supplies of waste material and wood were being transported to the beacon sites during the days before the lighting; in Crawley, Sussex, there was some criticism about the use of wood for the bonfire which could have been given to the town's senior citizens as fuel to keep their houses warm. This brought a rejoinder from the area manager of the pallet firm who had supplied the wood to the effect that he had between 6,000 and 7,000 broken pallets in his timber yard which anyone was welcome to have if they could collect them. The chairman of the local Festival committee made it clear that they had used "clean" material on the bonfire rather than rubbish, as had been suggested, to reduce air pollution, and said his committee had made an offer to old people to provide wood for them for the winter.

It would have been ironic if a campaign declaring war on moral pollution had contravened existing regulations governing environmental pollution, so in many cases where a bonfire beacon was not permissible the organizers had to turn to some alternative. The Leicester Festival committee found the answer—gas. The local Calor Gas sales and service centre spent a considerable time experimenting to produce a prototype large, ragged yellow flame on top of a six-foot pedestal. On the trial run the engineer was congratulated on his efforts and responded that it was the first time he had ever been commended for such an awful gas flame. It was subsequently tested by the Chief Fire Officer and a police inspector who satisfied themselves as to its safety. A bright flame two foot in diameter and six to seven feet high was produced, for a total cost of £25. The other local organizers were told of Leicester's success and were urged to contact their local Calor Gas sales and service centre to make the necessary arrangements.

The physical preparations for the beacons were only a small part of the total arrangements needing to be made for the local demonstrations in support of the Festival. Local churches had to be informed, speakers had to be booked and other local personalities encouraged to give their support. In some cases there was a ready-made Council of Churches or evangelistic committee to take up this work and use their existing networks to notify those in the area of what was taking place. In other cases the organizational work fell on the one or two individuals who felt most concerned about the issues involved and who—often working long hours during the two or three weeks at the beginning of September—wrote letters, visited people, made telephone calls, raised financial support, and liaised with the Festival headquarters when necessary.

Mrs. Doreen Cocking, of Sheffield, was not only responsible for organizing the beacon lighting in that city, but managed to do the whole thing in eight working days. She had written to the Festival headquarters in a private capacity asking for material to promote the Festival and was asked to organize the beacon lighting as a result of a telephone call from BBC Radio Sheffield to the London Festival's headquarters asking if Sheffield was taking part in the Festival. It was not, but Peter Hill went through the list of contacts they had in Sheffield, came across her name and telephoned to see if she could organize it. Considering the amount of time available to make the necessary arrangements it is surprising that she agreed to do it, but she says in retrospect, "It became more and more obvious to us during that week that God was organizing the Festival and we were just following Him." It seemed as though everyone was prepared to give the beacon lighting top priority, so that the police and city engineers gave verbal permission to the planned beacon without putting it before the necessary committee; the printer who at one stage adamantly refused to promise the posters in under a week, subsequently relented and pushed them through in two days, the Calor Gas manager at Leicester went to the expense of putting men on night shift and having parts for the beacon sent specially from Uxbridge and Dewsbury so that it could be ready in time.

In South Wales a letter was sent to nearly 1,000 churches, as result of which nineteen beacon sites were arranged, despite the fact that many of those contacted were already extremely busy in other areas of Christian work.

In the little village of Penn Street, near Amersham, in Buckinghamshire, it was originally intended that the local church should join with a group of churches from the Beaconsfield area at a bonfire to be lit on Beacon Hill, but the vicar reckoned without the enthusiasm of Oscar, a young "Hell's Angel" who had been converted two weeks before. He was indignant that there was to be no beacon in the village of Penn Street itself so the vicar said that if Oscar was prepared to build the beacon himself then he would arrange a service. Oscar was as good as his word and single-handed built a bonfire that was duly lit on the night of Operation Beacon and about thirty people stood around, including his parents. He helped to accompany the singing with his guitar, having learned the hymns and tunes from scratch and gave his testimony. Since the Festival he has managed to hold down a regular job for the first time and has started to work for his "O" Level Certificates at night school. For Oscar, says the vicar, the Festival was an opportunity to nail his colours firmly to the mast as a Christian.

Just how many beacons were lit on Thursday, September 23, no one will ever know. Peter Lyne, the organizer had details of at least 300 planned beacons and as far as is known, the majority of these plans came to fruition. Among the press cuttings that formed part of the material researched for this book there was documentary evidence of at least 270 beacons being lit. The first flame to leap skywards on that night should have been at Alexandra Palace, North London, but in fact it was probably at Hunsbury Hill, Northampton, where the lighting ceremony was brought forward by fifteen minutes to avoid the rain and to accommodate the waiting television cameramen. Nearly 300 people had gathered, despite the weather.

At Alexandra Palace disaster nearly struck. The beacon lighting there was to be tele-recorded for almost immediate transmission on the BBC's Nine o'clock News. A march of witness involving around 400 people from Ducketts Common arrived on the south terrace of the Palace to see the Calor Gas beacon being lit by Lord Longford. What the crowd, and the estimated 25 million television viewers did not know was that Nigel Goodwin, who was compéring the whole ceremony failed to arrive until five minutes before it was due to start, having been rushed from London Airport by car following a delayed flight from Scotland.

Cliff Richard who was appearing that month at the Fiesta Club in Sheffield appeared briefly in the city's Charter Square to light the beacon. He just had time to say, "But now most important of all is to keep it burning in our hearts", before returning to the club for his performance. Around 500 people had gathered in the Square, many of them with blazing torches. As far as is known the northernmost beacon in Great Britain was at Dundee, where the War Memorial beacon on the Law was lit for the first time since the Coronation. Around 300 marchers, including a group of young people waving a banner inscribed "Home rule for Jesus", made the half mile climb from the city to the Law, the highest point overlooking Dundee.

There was a positive rash of beacons in Devon and Cornwall estimated at between fifty and seventy in all. The farthest west were those at Marazion beach and Lariggan Rocks, Penzance. At the eastern tip of the country there was a march through the town of Great Yarmouth by sixty members of local churches together with the Salvation Army band. A fifteen foot long pillar of light which had been carried at the head of the marchers was burned on the beach near the jetty.

In the Bristol area there were twelve beacons ringing the city, only one of which had to be specifically arranged by the regional co-ordinator, the remaining eleven were arranged spontaneously, attended by a total of over 3,000 people. The Leicester beacon, about nine miles from the city itself, at Woodhouse Eaves, was supported by churches throughout the area and attended by around 2,000 people, including the Bishop of Leicester and the Archdeacon of Loughborough. A similar number attended the beacon lighting at Swansea, despite the fact that preparations only got under way during the last fortnight before the event. At Penarth, farther along the South Wales coast, there was a great deal of controversy and opposition from local authority officials who were members of the "Clean Air Society", but this did not stop the beacon eventually being lit. More than 200 people marched through the town with torches to the site. At Pontyprydd the Chairman of the Council lit three torches on the steps of the town hall which were then taken by runners through the streets to light three beacons, one in the centre of the town and two others on hills either side of the town where groups were praying.

A crowd of 300 climbed to the top of Warden Hill, Luton, to see the beacon being lit. The torch to light the beacon was carried by six relay runners from the town hall where they were lit by the deputy mayor. Unfortunately his lighter spluttered and refused to light, but a nearby clergyman produced an old fashioned box of matches and saved the day. The bonfire on Barr Beacon was the result of plans first discussed at a meeting arranged by Dr. Robert Browne, the doctor who, as mentioned earlier, was cleared by the General Medical Council of professional misconduct over his decision to tell the parents of a sixteen year old girl that she was on the Pill.

Several beacons encountered opposition. Groups of counter-demonstrators infiltrated the march of witness at Stevenage distributing *Oz* literature. Vandals struck at a church in Swindon before the town's beacon was lit. Slogans were daubed on tombstones and a fire was started in the churchyard. Firemen brought it under control before it reached the oil tanks which housed the fuel for the church's heating system. At Derry Hill, near Chippenham, the beacon was fired by hooligans several hours before it was due to be lit. Church officials hastily prepared another bonfire. At Rochdale, the White Panthers, a hippy group, caused some trouble, whilst at Canterbury swearing and heckling accompanied the beacon-lighting ceremony.

The uncertainties of the English climate played havoc with surprisingly few of the arrangements for beacon lighting. Though many areas had heavy rain during the day and early evening on September 23, very few beacon lighting ceremonies had to be called off or re-arranged. At Winterbourne, just outside Bristol, the bonfire was sited close to an embankment covered with tinder dry grass which caused the organizers considerable anxiety in case sparks should set fire to it all. However heavy rain in the afternoon completely dampened the offending grass, though it cleared in time for the actual ceremony. Well over a hundred people braved a downpour of rain and swirling mists on the Worcestershire Beacon where the beacon was so successful that many calls were made to the police and the proprietor of the nearby restaurant on the assumption that the Beacon Café was on fire. Hove firemen were called to Portslade, Sussex, to dowse the flames from the beacon when police feared they were getting out of control.

Searchlights shone into the night sky above Plymouth Hoe where thousands took part in an open air rally addressed by the Rev. Paul Tucker which preceded the bonfire lighting. Other members of the Council of Reference were also pressed into service to light beacons. Malcolm Muggeridge was at Hastings, together with 1,000 others for the town's beacon-lighting. At Portsdown Hill, Portsmouth, 1,200 people made do with the next best thing—a Muggeridge tape recording. David Kossoff, the actor, was at Crystal Palace where the bonfire was helped to blaze by sixty old armchairs used as fuel. Among other speakers present were an ex-pornography pedlar who said that since his conversion to Christianity it had taken more than three years to kill his mind of the effects of his work. Ted Lyons, the young East Ender who spoke at the Festival's inaugural rally, and George Verwer, director of Operation Mobilization, with which Peter Hill worked in India also took part. Col. Dobbie and his daughter Carol spoke to a crowd of about 1,000 in church before they moved out to light the beacon. Eddie Stride was on home ground that evening, speaking at St. Matthias Church, Poplar, before the bonfire lighting ceremony in the churchyard. Peter Hill was at Southborough where 400 people from Tonbridge and Tunbridge Wells held two torchlight processions culminating in the beacon-lighting. An opposition group started their own fire on the site but it was quickly extinguished. Another 250 attended the beacon at nearby Sevenoaks. Ernest Shippam was at Amberley

Mount, together with 500 people from the Chichester and Bognor Regis areas to light one of several beacons in and around West Sussex.

Mr. John Biggs Davidson, Member of Parliament for Chigwell, was one of several MP's who identified themselves with the Festival. He sent a message to the beacon-lighting at St. John's Church, Buckhurst Hill, in which he said, "It is not so much a permissive society as a licentious, callous and cruel society, perhaps even a doomed society. Too many films, whether in the uncensored film club or elsewhere are blue, sadistic, subversive or all three. Parents are often at a loss for entertainment. Nudity, not for art but for kicks, blasphemy and simulated sex acts have won the freedom of the stage. The Christian strives to imitate Christ who calls him, married or not, to heroic purity. May the Festival of Light radiate the Light of the World".

Chingford (Essex) beacon-lighters chose a site once used by a witches' coven for their bonfire. At Horsenden Hill, in the north west suburbs of London, television personality Bob Danvers Walker had some harsh things to say about the media: "I have been in broadcasting, radio and television for forty five years, including thirty years in cinema newsreels and never in that time would I have thought the day would dawn when it would be found necessary for people to rise up in righteous indignation at the way licentiousness, obscenity, pornography and depravity are commonplace and smeared over so much of what is salaciously called popular entertainment. This is the age when men with dirty minds and tongues flourish because up till now there has been no militancy against those degenerates who befoul every form of art and even education. This Festival and those who support it have taken up the cudgels to stop the rot."

Plans for a beacon at Brynmawr in Breconshire, the highest town in Wales, were drawn up rather late—two days before the appointed date, in fact. A site was agreed with the local authority, police and fire brigade and local industries were asked to dump any inflammable material or rubbish they might have on the site on Thursday morning.

Just as the first lorry-load of rubbish was due to be tipped a gas board workman appeared on the scene: "Hey, you can't tip it there for a bonfire; you're on top of a gas main!" Accordingly the rubbish was tipped a few yards away. The second lorry was about to deliver a load of wood when along came a farmer: "You can't tip it there; you'll be in my way. There'll be trouble if one of my sheep eats a plastic bag." The site was moved for the second time, to a hillock a short distance beyond. Just before the third lorry tipped its load of old tyres on to the pile of wood, two more farmers turned up. In fairly colourful language they made it known that they were from the Commoners Association and a bonfire on that site was out of the question. Sadly the clergyman directing the operation had to send the lorry-load of tyres back where it came from and divert several other lorries scheduled to deliver more rubbish.

As the crowds began to gather at 8.30 p.m. that evening their path to what was to have been the bonfire was blocked by a tractor and van placed there by the Commoners—who were also in attendance—and most of them turned back. In explaining to those who remained the reason for the cancellation, the local Baptist pastor provoked the Commoners to an angry reply. It was, as someone remarked, not so much a Festival of Light, more a Festival of Heat. The Commoners insisted that the rubbish be cleared before the morning, so with bare hands the faithful few piled the rotting refuse back into a lorry procured at remarkably short notice. They finished their task well after midnight and proved beyond reasonable doubt that they were prepared to tackle more than just one sort of pollution.

One of the smallest recorded attendances at any beacon was at Farnham-Royal Rectory, near Slough, where only eight people including the rector were present. By contrast the beacon on the Hogs Back, near Guildford, drew a crowd in excess of 2,000. Two members of the Executive Committee were present at beacons in the London area, Jean Darnall at Watford and Bernard Madden at Harlow, whilst Nick Cuthbert was at Derby.

The objective of Operation Beacon was to confront the

nation with a warning in the same manner as the beacons announcing the Spanish Armada had been a warning. Many of the speakers at the beacons spoke to their brief referring to an "invasion of moral pollution". Some local press reports took the warning aspect to be the total message of the Festival, but this was unavoidable. There is, after all, little point in talking about the need for light if people cannot recognize the fact of darkness.

If it is not possible to know exactly how many beacons were lit it is even more difficult to assess the total number of people present at the various beacons around the country. Information available through press cuttings of nearly half the beacons suggest that the final total would be somewhere in the region of 100,000 people. So on a damp, but ultimately fine night, as the gas beacons were abruptly turned off and as the bonfires blazed with varying degrees of brightness through the night the first part of Jean Darnall's vision came true. Throughout the country from north to south, from east to west, the lights were lit. In two days' time, those lights were, metaphorically speaking, to converge on London to complete her vision and at the same time to fulfil the vision given to Peter Hill some nine months earlier.

Chapter Five

AND THERE WAS LIGHT

DESPITE ALL that the cynics and critics may have said, may be saying, and may continue to say, after the events in Trafalgar Square on September 25, London will never be the same again. After the long months of planning and preparation and the hectic weeks of frenzied activity, it happened. The Festival of Light was no longer a vision. It was a reality. During the final few weeks before September 25 while the regional rallies and last-minute preparations for beacon-lightings were going on around the country, the Executive Committee, their sub-committees, the full-time staff and all their young helpers were busy putting the finishing touches to preparations for the great London rallies.

The Trafalgar Square rally was mainly Eddy Stride's responsibility. He had gathered together a team of speakers which "partially organized, partially providential" as he says, were a remarkable cross-section of society. Lord Beswick, Chief Labour Whip in the House of Lords and Mrs. Peggy Fenner, a Conservative MP; George Goyder, managing director of a large paper company and Frank Deeks, a left-wing shop steward; Bill Davidson, a young Salvation Army officer, and Mrs. Monica Commerford, a Roman Catholic housewife; David Kossoff, a Jew, famous as an actor, and Nick Cuthbert, an evangelical student; with Malcolm Muggeridge, Mary Whitehouse and members of the Executive Committee, these all made a very strong line-up.

Music was to be provided by the Salvation Army in the shape of the Good News guitar group, successors to the famous Joystrings, and three bands, the Regent Hall Band, who were to lead the singing in the Square, the Youth band and a composite band who were to lead and support the March of Witness. (The Festival committee had discovered by this time that the Salvation Army had been working along similar lines to the Festival during the year. They had canvassed 50,000 signatures in support of a petition calling on the "governmental and broadcasting authorities as well as press and arts councils to use their powers in stemming the present pollution of mass pornography infecting books, magazines, newspapers, theatres, cinemas, radio and television". The signatures, collected in a very short space of time, indicated "the strength of feeling in a large part of society against the commercialization of sex in ways which ensure financial gain for the exploiters and the creation of false values in the lives of the exploited". As evidence of Salvation Army support for the Festival, Commissioner Albert Mingay, leader of the Army in the United Kingdom, was subsequently present on the platform at the Square.

Two people who played a major part in preparations for the Trafalgar Square rally were Henry Hole, who had been chief steward at the Billy Graham crusades, and Phil Golledge, a solicitor's clerk from Worthing, who had offered his services to Peter Hill after he heard him speak about the Festival at one of the Abinger Convention meetings at Dorking earlier in the summer. Between them they had been responsible for making all the necessary arrangements, meeting officials of the Department of The Environment and the police, organizing such mundane but necessary details as the erection of the platform, the installation of the public address system, the recruiting and training of marshals and so on. Golledge's industry seemed untiring.

The proclamations to be read out in the Square to the Government, the media and the Church, drafts of which had been discussed at length by committee members and other advisers, had still not been finalized ten days before the rally. At one of the final committee meetings, four drafts of various lengths were read aloud and discussed after which it was decided that there should be three separate proclamations of between 250 and 300 words each, with positive content and including constructive suggestions. Gordon Landreth continued working on them with a small committee and eventually they were ready by the Sunday before the rally. One advantage of their late preparation was that they could take account of developments right up to the last minute. There had been strong requests from some religious newspapers to have copies of the proclamations in time to print them in the issues of their papers published during the week in which the London rallies took place. There was a feeling that otherwise those present at Trafalgar Square would be committing themselves in advance without knowing what the proclamations contained. The committee agreed to release summaries of the proclamations to the press for publication from Thursday morning onwards and to print 20,000 copies of the summaries for distribution by the stewards in Trafalgar Square.

The Hyde Park rally was in its way a much bigger

operation than Trafalgar Square, and it had a much more chequered history. When Col. Dobbie and Phil Golledge, who was as much involved in the Park rally as he was with the one in the Square, first went to see officials of the Department of The Environment it appeared as though a door was being slammed in their faces. No amplification permitted, no distribution of leaflets, severe limitation on the duration of the rally. Only a miracle, it seemed, could save the situation, but the miracle happened, and the rally went ahead more or less as planned with the full approval and support of the authorities.

Nigel Goodwin had been made responsible for the Park rally in the early days of the committee. Despite his many contacts in the field of music and the arts, his attempts to get together a top-line display of artists for the rally met with only limited success. It was not until Gordon Scutt, a young insurance broker in the City, was brought in to join him that things really started to move. He was a member of the committee of the Stewards Trust, a group which provided a forum for Christians who lived in the country but worked and stayed in London during the week. He was therefore in direct contact with a large number of people who were subsequently able to give valuable support to the Festival.

Fortunately Gordon Scutt was able to devote all his energies—and almost all his time—to the Hyde Park rally during the four weeks that elapsed between his co-option on to the committee on August 25 and the Festival itself. His first job was to try for some of the big names in the world of popular music who might be prepared to appear. Pat Boone, Johnny Cash and Mahalia Jackson were some of those mentioned in the course of a long trans-Atlantic 'phone call he had with Bill Brown, of the Billy Graham Evangelistic Association, but none of them was available. Lovelace Watkins was in London appearing in Cabaret, but Scutt got no further than his manager. Dana, the Irish singer who won the 1970 Eurovision Song Contest, and Terry Dene, who had been a rock and roll sensation back in the late fifties, had already agreed to come. Dana, a Roman

Catholic, believed in the evangelistic aims of the Hyde Park rally; Terry Dene, who was converted in the mid-sixties, was working as a full-time evangelist. Cliff Richard, although fully in sympathy with the Festival, was rather reluctant at first to appear at the concert as he did not want to "hog the limelight" as he put it.

Two American music groups were also secured, the Forerunners, who had been a great success at British concerts organized during the previous few years by Musical Gospel Outreach, and Country Faith, one of the best Jesus People groups. The latter group were flown over from Sweden, where they were touring, as a result of Lonnie Frisbee's participation in the inaugural rally at Westminster Central Hall. He had been so impressed with the meeting and the idea behind the Festival that he recommended that Country Faith be invited to take part in the Hyde Park rally. Gordon Giltrap, recognized as one of the leading guitarists in the country and a newly converted Christian, Judy Mackenzie and Graham Kendrick, both popular performers at MGO concerts, completed the musical side of the rally.

The team of speakers represented a number of different traditions. The Rev. Tony Sargent, was minister of Worthing Tabernacle and a member of the Westminster Fellowship. Jean Darnall came from within the American Pentecostal tradition. The Rev. David Watson was a young Anglican clergyman from York who had taken over a church there which had been declared redundant and seen it grow until it was bursting at the seams. The Rev. David MacInnes, precentor of Birmingham Cathedral, had been among the first to know about the Festival at the beginning of the year. Two young people were to be interviewed by Nigel Goodwin, the compére: Ted Lyons, who took part in the Festival's inaugural rally, and Alison Fraser-Skemp, the young actress who played the part of Mary Tudor in the successful BBC television series *The Six Wives of Henry the Eighth.*

And then there was Arthur Blessitt. An itinerant leader of the American Jesus Movement, he came to Britain at the beginning of September 1971 with the declared intention of carrying a wooden cross from London to Belfast and there setting it up between the warring factions, as they then were, of Protestants and Roman Catholics. On the way he engaged in "street evangelism"—talking to people about Jesus and distributing stickers and literature to passers-by.

He first became involved with the Festival when Col. Dobbie visited a "pop" concert with some committee members to "see how it was done". Blessitt was there in the crowd surrounded by young people talking about Jesus. Col. Dobbie approached him there and then, as a result of which Blessitt agreed to meet Gordon Scutt. Following this he attended a meeting arranged to discuss follow-up and counselling at the rally. After sitting quietly through most of the meeting he later held those present spell-bound as he outlined what he would do in a situation like Hyde Park. It was clear from this that he would have to take part in the rally at some point, and though he had to fly back to America for a television appearance on the Monday before the Festival, he returned the same day and was present at the Park to give the closing talk.

Publicity for the rally took the form of thousands of stickers bearing the legend "Smile, Jesus loves you. Hyde Park, September 25, 4 p.m." Groups of young people "invaded" a "pop" concert held on the famous Oval cricket ground in London distributing the stickers, and even the more staid and respectable members of the Executive Committee are known to have stuck them on every available lamp-post, telephone kiosk and bus-stop they could find. On the Saturday before the Festival, Arthur Blessitt was in Trafalgar Square with a crowd of young people witnessing to Jesus and inviting people to Hyde Park the following week. Follow-up literature for the rally was produced in the form of a leaflet containing on one side a contemporary cartoon telling the story of Jesus healing the blind man and on the other an up-to-date version of John Chapter 8, entitled, "Personal Freedom: Jesus Christ and the system", together with a selection of London telephone numbers where further help could be obtained.

1. Steve Stevens (left) and Peter Hill. *Photo : Clifford Shirley*

2. (above) The scene at the Blackheath (South London) beacon. (below) Bishop Trevor Huddleston speaking at the Fleet Street press conference. *Photos : Clifford Shirley*

3. (above) Malcolm Muggeridge speaking at Trafalgar Square. (below) A section of the Trafalgar Square crowd. *Photos: Clifford Shirley*

4. The crowd in Trafalgar Square – "The Silent Majority finds its voice." *Photo : Clifford Shirley*

5. (above) The start of the march to Hyde Park. *Photo : Clifford Shirley*. (below) A section of the Hyde Park crowd – an estimated 60,000 attended. *Photo : Camera Press Ltd.*

6. Cliff Richard lights the Sheffield beacon. *Photo: Sheffield Newspapers Ltd.*

7. (above) Volunteers help at the Woodford 'headquarters'. *Photo: Clifford Shirley.* (below) Dora Bryan and Arthur Blessitt at the Manchester Festival of Light which was televised. *Photo: E. K. Thomson*

8. (above) An 'opposition' protester is escorted away from the Hyde Park crowd. *Photo : Clifford Shirley*. (below) The Bishop of Manchester lights the Manchester flame. *Photo : E. K. Thomson*

Elaborate security arrangements were felt to be necessary in view of the experience at the inaugural rally and rumours which were circulating at that time about possible stronger opposition at the rallies on September 25. An article in *The Guardian* of September 11 quoted one organizer of Operation Rupert (the "code name" for the Central Hall protest) as saying they would be mounting various events in Hyde Park and wanted to involve as many people as possible. "People should be able to get both points of view and we hope they will see us as sincere, intelligent, worried people and not the devils we are made out to be." The Festival of Life, as it was to be called, would be a "celebration of human non-violent joy. We want to be humorous and serious at the same time. We feel it strongly that the real obscenities—half a million children starving now in India—should be put forward."

Among the literature circulated by the underground press was a facsimile of the Operation Beacon announcement with dates and several other details changed, backed on the reverse of the sheet by a take-off of the event headlined, "Nationwide Festival of Life". Parodying the language used on the official announcement about the beacon lighting, it claimed that "during the past two decades racial discrimination, political repression, the obscenity of British justice, the systematic corruption of the young by our establishment schools has been eroding the moral fibre of this once great planet". At one time the estimated support for the opposition's Festival of Life was given as 10,000 and it was undoubtedly because of these stories and the experience at the inaugural rally, that the police took the precaution of ferrying coach-loads of policemen to the sites of the rallies.

For their own part, the Hyde Park rally organizers took steps to guard as far as possible against the platform being rushed. There was to be only one entrance to the compound at the rear of the platform which would be double-fenced, and at least forty marshals were to patrol the compound area. Marshals were to be closely and thoroughly checked to guard against bogus marshals disrupting plans. The platform was to be carefully inspected early on the

Saturday morning and no television or press personnel were to be allowed in the compound or on the platform.

Work was still continuing at the Festival headquarters at the same hectic pace which had characterized the last few days before the inaugural rally. A final circular was sent to all the regional co-ordinators with precise instructions as to travelling arrangements, loading and unloading of coach passengers and timing of arrivals and departures in London. Those coming by train were warned that they would not be permitted to march from the station to Trafalgar Square nor to display any banners.

In an illuminating paragraph on the probability of opposition groups at the London rallies, Col. Dobbie had this to say: "After the Central Hall meeting many conversations were carried on with those who had sought to interrupt the meeting and as individuals they were found to be nice, but unhappy and confused people who thought that both we as individuals and the Church rejected them. What a cause for repentance at our obvious lack of love." He urged those coming to London to "seek out these others and talk with them and above all listen to them individually as fellow sinners for whom Christ died". Those attending the rallies were asked not to carry slogans, which it was suggested were always a sign of protest, but instead to have placards and banners along the lines recommended by the Festival organizers, together with others stating where they were from.

The limited space available at the Eastwood Road premises was tested to the full by the arrival of 2,000 white T-shirts with the orange beacon flame on the front. The idea had come to Steve Stevens quite suddenly one evening, and he had managed to find a manufacturer who could give him a speedy delivery date. In order to notify Festival supporters about the T-shirts, give them a reminder about the Nationwide Day of Prayer, the beacon-lightings and the London rallies, and tell them about the Festival's launching rally at the Central Hall, Steve decided that a complete mailing should be done to all the 3,000–4,000 addresses on the list. Once more the addressing of envelopes had to be shared around voluntary groups in the area and all other activity was suspended in order to speed the collating, folding and inserting of material into envelopes. So great was the crush inside the house that trestle tables had to be put up in the garden on which the MAF folding machine, loaned for the occasion, was put. Fortunately it was a fine hot day, so the idea was quite popular.

Had Steve and Peter realized earlier the size of the task to which they had set their hands they would probably have said in despair, "It can't be done". That it was done was remarkable and due in part to the atmosphere somewhere between that of a revival meeting and a holiday camp, which permeated the Festival headquarters from dawn to dusk. Complete informality, casual dress, "Hallelujah" and "Praise the Lord" the most frequent utterances, spontaneous bursts of song, non-stop humour and leg-pulling, vivacious high spirits bubbling over (a photograph of a typically grim-looking Emperor Hirohito was put up on one of the doors with a sticker underneath it, "Smile, Jesus loves you"), this was the formula for success. Everyday time was set aside for prayer, and there is no doubt that the whole experience was an exuberant one for young and old alike.

There was an air of subdued excitement at the final Executive Committee meeting held on the Tuesday before the great day. There was a full attendance of all those who had been involved in the various stages of the planning and preparation for the Festival, including several of the wives of committee members and other helpers. They listened intently as Col. Dobbie read some verses from 1 John 1: 5–7: "This is the message we have heard from Him and proclaim to you, that God is light and in Him is no darkness at all. If we say we have fellowship with Him while we walk in darkness, we lie and do not live according to the truth; but if we walk in the light as He is in the light we have fellowship with one another, and the blood of Jesus Christ His son cleanses us from all sin." (RSV). He went on to read two verses from Nehemiah 6: 15–16, which several people had remarked upon earlier, since the Festival was to take place on the

25th day of the month: "So the wall was finished on the 25th day of the Elul (the Hebrew word for September!) in fifty two days. And when all our enemies heard of it all the nations round about us were afraid and fell greatly in their own esteem; for they perceived that this work had been acomplished with the help of our God." (RSV).

After a time of prayer there was prolonged and full discussion of various matters relating to the arrangements for Saturday's rallies. The police, who were planning for a crowd of 30,000, were convinced that their arrangements were such that the platform in Trafalgar Square could not be rushed. Col. Dobbie was asked to send a telegram of appreciation and thanks to the police and also telegrams from the Council of Reference and the Executive Committee to the Queen and the Prince of Wales conveying their "loyalty and humble duty". As the discussion continued and points were noted or actions recommended, more than one committee member must have felt that in one sense all these final details were insignificant. They had been conscious, during the previous few weeks in particular, that God seemed to be over-ruling the whole project. Their own slender resources had been stretched to the limit and, like the loaves and fishes of old, multiplied time and again to achieve results out of all proportion to their original size.

Each man and woman sitting round the table in the back room of Spitalfield's rectory that evening had brought to the committee differing gifts and varied experience. They were also of diverse temperament and personality, some blunt and outspoken, others tactful and persuasive, and yet at no time did they ever have to take a vote on any issue. Different views might be expressed but a common mind would emerge. Part of the reason for this impressive spirit of give and take was due to the fact that each committee member left his status at the door when he went in, so that the director of a large property company, dealing with millions of pounds a day, could humbly learn from the solicitor's clerk concerned with the daily routine of the legal machine. But the major reason was undoubtedly because "they all with one accord devoted themselves to prayer". Seldom did their meetings contain less than forty minutes spent praying for their common concerns, and like the Early Church they experienced their deepest moments of fellowship in prayer. To adapt an old adage, "The committee which prays together, stays together".

After nearly five hours of discussion and prayer the final committee meeting ended at quarter past eleven. As the committee members walked out into the dingy streets of London's East End they must have wondered what experiences they would each have to recount to each other when next they met.

On the following day positively the last circular was dispatched from the Festival office to regional co-ordinators with last minute instructions about beacon lightings, proclamations, T-shirts, banners and hymn-sheets. By way of emphasizing the positive nature of the effort, those to whom the letter was sent were urged to contact the BBC to comment favourably on Bishop Huddleston's talk that morning on the radio programme *Thought for the Day*.

On the Friday before the Festival Peter Thompson had a telephone call from a sub-editor on the *Sunday Mirror* asking why the Festival had been called off. Apparently a 'phone message purporting to come from Thompson had been received by the *Mirror* saying that the Festival had been cancelled. He quickly checked round a few more papers and found they had had similar messages. It was a rather weak effort by the opposition, as they must have realized that the message would be checked back with its supposed source before anything was published. But as an extra safeguard Thompson arranged that any future message would only be considered genuine if his middle name, which was almost certainly unknown to anyone in the opposition, was given by the informant. That was not the only hoax perpetrated by opponents of the Festival. Many letters were sent out on Wednesday and Thursday to some who were organizing coach parties and making other arrangements to bring people to the Trafalgar Square rally saying that due to overcrowding in the Square, their group should bypass the first rally and go straight to the Hyde

Park rally which would not now start until 6 p.m. A quick telephone call to the Festival office would have confirmed that the letter was a fraud, and news of the hoax letters was given in several papers, so it is unlikely that many people were deceived.

Also on Friday, Col. Dobbie received Prince Charles' acknowledgement of the telegram sent earlier in the week on behalf of the Festival. To his delight he saw that it was more than just a formal reply. It concluded with the words, "With every good wish for the success of the Festival". Immediately he tried to contact the Prince's Equerry to see if it would be in order to pass on his good wishes to the crowd in the Square. The Equerry could not be traced but —after consideration—Dobbie decided to break the news.

Saturday morning dawned cool and grey. Peter Hill was woken by a telephone call at 6.15 a.m. from the first contingent of Festival supporters to arrive in London, all the way from North Wales. Should they all come down to South Woodford, they wanted to know, or stay where they were? They were soon joined by others from Cornwall who had travelled through the night. The office staff set out for Trafalgar Square in an old ten hundredweight van loaned for the day, packed full of T-shirts, banners, posters, badges and literature. They arrived at about ten o'clock and parked the van close by the plinth on the west side. A prayer meeting was held in the Bridewell Hall, Victoria, from ten o'clock onwards and nearly 600 stewards gathered at St. Martin-in-the-Fields for briefing about the role they were to play in Trafalgar Square and Hyde Park. They were not simply to patrol the "forbidden areas" and keep an eye open for trouble. They were to act as guides, "information centres" and, if necessary as counsellors to any who needed them.

By eleven o'clock it was clear that there was going to be a very large crowd indeed. Young people were already packed against the steel barrier fencing off the area in front of the scaffolding platform by the plinth. There was a continuous queue of young people at the mobile headquarters, wanting more literature and posters to distribute amongst their friends and give to bystanders, including bus drivers and taxi drivers who were passing round the Square, with the greeting, "God bless you, Hallelujah". Many of those present had obviously come up to London for the day and were using the morning for sightseeing, coming to the Square round about lunchtime, and between 12 o'clock and two o'clock there was much coming and going as the Square gradually filled up and movement across the wide expanse between the two fountains became more difficult.

It was a heterogeneous cross-section of society. There were elderly people sitting on the benches around the perimeter of the Square, many of them in their sixties and seventies, there were middle-aged mothers and fathers with their families, there were young married couples with babes in arms and young children, but chiefly there were the young people. Right from the start young people out-numbered all the other age groups put together. They were not the sort of young person who might have been identified with such an open air rally five years ago, soberly dressed with neat hair styles and solemn faces. These young people were vibrant, enthusiastic, gaily dressed and above all—happy. Long hair, short hair, jeans, trouser-suits, mini skirts, maxi skirts—they were all there. A score of spontaneous choirs accompanied by their own guitars started up around the Square as the crowd got bigger.

One and a half miles across London, at Hyde Park, around this time, an incident occurred which could have had significant repercussions. To obtain sufficient power for the level of amplification necessary in view of the expected crowd, 2,000 watts were required, whereas the equipment available had a maximum output of 1,200 watts. How could the extra power be made up? As the members of the Hyde Park committee were thinking and praying about this a van drew up alongside the compound. The driver, together with two companions had apparently been engaged by one of the rival *Oz* bands to provide amplification for them in opposition to the Festival, but he said that on his way into London "an overwhelming conviction" came over them that they "were on the wrong side and should be supporting the Festival, not opposing it". His equipment amounted to 400 watts of extra power—half of what was needed.

This put the organizers in something of a quandary. Here was half an answer to their prayers but. . . . Suppose it was a hoax or an attempt to disrupt the proceedings in some way? Their problem was solved when it was found that the *Oz* equipment would not "blend" with what they already had, so the offer was declined. As it turned out the existing 1,200 watts of power proved more than adequate. But the incident was told and retold again so many times in the course of the next few weeks that it became almost apocryphal and in its extreme form gave the impression that had it not been for the *Oz* man's offer there would have been no amplification at the Festival meetings at all!

Back in the Square people were flooding in from all sides, and as the available space in the Square itself filled up so they spilled over on to the steps, the pavement, and into the entrance to the National Gallery across the road to the north of the Square. Each of the marshals had been given copies of the summaries of the proclamations to be read out, together with hymn sheets, and they, together with Christian newspaper and magazine sellers were edging through the crowds. At 2.30 p.m. the VIPs emerged from St. Martin-in-the-Fields, made their way across to the plinth and mounted the steps to be greeted with rousing cheers from the onlookers. Since 2 p.m. the Good News Group had been giving some official accompaniment and eventually, leadership in the spontaneous singing which rose from the crowd. Although the afternoon rally had been advertised to start at three o'clock, it was felt, in view of the time it would take for the march to Hyde Park, that if the Square was full by half past two a start should be made then.

It was in fact at about 2.40 p.m. when Eddy Stride stepped forward to the microphone, welcomed the vast crowd to the meeting and explained the purpose of the rally. It was somehow fitting that Malcolm Muggeridge should be the first speaker. Perhaps more than any other public figure he had been identified with the Festival throughout and though he spoke for only a few minutes he undoubtedly set the tone for the rest of the proceedings. "Fellow celebrants of the Festival of Light, for those who have been concerned in mounting this demonstration for Christ this is a very great moment," he said. "I look round with pride and joy at all these faces, at all these banners and this mighty turn-out and pray with all my heart that it may be the beginning of a continuing process of moral and spiritual regeneration.

"Speaking particularly for myself, but I think for the rest of you too, the mood induced in me by the Festival experience has been one of deep humility and an abiding sense of being so in need of salvation myself that any tendency to censoriousness or self-righteousness has seemed totally inadmissible. It has been for me an immense clarification. I see more clearly than ever before that the many problems and dilemmas which confront twentieth century man arise out of one thing—his attempt to live without God. An attempt which leads on the one hand into the fantasies which go with imagining that he is a god himself and on the other into the squalid abyss of a reversion to animality, megalomania and erotomania. We know and we proclaim that without God we are irretrievably lost in the darkness of our mortality and we turn to Christ our Saviour the Light of the World."

Applause which had punctuated his address at regular intervals became deafening at this stirring proclamation. He concluded: "The Light of the World to light the way to His Kingdom where God reigns—this is our message. This is the light of our Festival of Light. Praise the Lord."

After Captain Bill Davidson, of the Salvation Army, had spoken Eddy Stride came to the microphone.

"And now, a message from another young man who lives not so far from here," he said. Col. Dobbie read out Prince Charles's message and a great cheer echoed round the Square when he came to the last sentence. Peter Hill introduced Judy Mackenzie to the audience and she led the great crowd in the now famous Festival song.

Mrs. Mary Whitehouse brought greetings from sympathizers in New Zealand, America, Germany, Australia, France and Canada, and a message from the director of the Danish Cultural Institute, who said "There is no doubt that what is happening here today will greatly strengthen the Danish Government". She also brought a personal message from the Pope who had told her he would remember the Festival in his personal prayers. He was, she said, "tremendously encouraged by the efforts we are making here in Britain".

Frank Deeks, the Dagenham shop steward, came forward to accuse the media, the government and the churches. "We ordinary people have allowed, through apathy, our television sets to become sewers; our cinemas cess-pools; our children to be exposed to corrupt teaching," he said. "Our newspapers print the lurid, the violent, the depraved, the sensational and often downright filth. Our Parliament, Lords and Commons, Government and Opposition have failed to give moral leadership and have often capitulated for squalid party gain. Our Churches (and may God forgive us) have often been compromising, hesitant and plain scared to give a lead. Vast fortunes were being made by men who were manipulating the misplaced idealism of many young people. 'Stop all censorship and the people will tire of pornography' was their cry. The last time they told us that was about gambling so we allowed betting shops and casinos. Now we have a huge gambling industry sapping the nation's strength and rich men are getting richer by it. We must not repeat that mistake."

Mrs. Monica Cummerford, mother of five children and a columnist in the *Catholic Herald*, spoke of the society in which she wanted her family to develop and grow. During this time the audience were good humouredly applauding the speakers, and occasionally lapsing into shouts of "J-E-S-U-S" and "Hallelujah". There appeared to be little or no disruption from the opposition, except two or three smoke bombs thrown into the crowd. On one occasion when the television camera crews spotted a smoke bomb they swung the cameras round and zoomed in on the action. But by that time Festival supporters in front of the bomb had raised their banners high to form a shield, and all that appeared on the TV screens of the incident was row upon row of Festival posters.

It was obvious that the public address system, efficient though it was for the majority of the crowd present, could not be heard by everybody within the Square, particularly those who were behind the huge loudspeakers directed towards the most populous parts of the Square. But everybody was able to keep in touch with what was happening by joining every now and then in verses from "Onward Christian Soldiers".

In the mobile headquarters by the side of the plinth the supply of T-shirts was coming to an end. Rather than close shop when the rally started Kay Stevens and her helpers had continued serving, thinking it would be a pity to disappoint those who were still waiting. One of the last customers was a little old Irish lady, who pointed to a jersey one of the helpers had hung up inside the van, saying, "And how much is that blue jersey up there?" She obviously thought it was a jumble sale! After the last T-shirt had gone there was still one girl who was very disappointed not to have one. Kay suddenly thought of an answer. Steve had got his original T-shirt dirty and had changed into a clean one. "I've got a dirty one here I'll give you for 25p", she said to the girl. "Do you want it?" The girl was delighted and went off quite content in Steve's dirty shirt.

The last T-shirt gone they left the van and climbed on to the plinth. As Kay joined her husband with the platform party she recalls that she went "cold with thrill". "All I could see was a sea of young faces. I wouldn't have swopped that sight for a month's luxury holiday anywhere in the world. To think that the Lord allowed our humble home to be used for this."

Lord Beswick, Chief Labour Whip in the House of Lords, came to the microphone to speak as a politician on the general problem of moral pollution. "I have never in my experience seen a demonstration in this Square that is more meaningful or more potentially important, or, as I look at all the young faces here below me, more hopeful than the one I see today." He pointed out that many earlier demonstrations protested against material poverty about which much had subsequently been done, but it was important that society learned how to use the leisure time that it had acquired. "I cannot believe that the great social reformers, the trade union and Labour struggles were struggles to eliminate poverty simply to make room for pornography."

He spoke of the call for personal liberty and individual freedom, but pointed out that liberty was too often being used for selfish, personal, profit seeking purposes. "Is it not true that many people are exploiting personal freedom for shoddy commercial purposes. If it is a question of individual people or companies producing shoddy garments or building shoddy houses, it is commonly agreed that their freedom should be curbed yet it seems that if people or companies produce shoddy books, or shoddy films, or shoddy newspapers, and sex is involved, there is a tendency to say that we should not interfere. Yet the motivation has nothing at all to do with artistic freedom or cultural expression. It is the same attempt to make money by selling a shoddy article."

Steve Stevens came forward to explain how the proclamations were compiled. He emphasized that they represented the views of the executive committee, but not necessarily those of speakers at the rally, who had been asked to speak "because of their known concern with the values of love, purity and family life, but not because of any known commitment to the executive committee's views on how to meet the threats to which these values are exposed at present." Before he returned to his place he asked all those under twenty five to raise their hands. A great cheer went up when it was seen that they accounted for around two-thirds of those present. Before Nick Cuthbert read the first proclamation Mrs. Peggy Fenner, Conservative Member of Parliament for Rochester and Chatham, said she had been "shocked and saddened as a wife and mother at trends which are assaulting the stability of family life," and feared that they had infiltrated the educational system.

The proclamation to the Government recognized the

dangers of the physical pollution of the environment, but expressed the belief that moral pollution presented an even greater danger. Health of mind, the value of the individual, concern for the underpriviledged, purity, love, the family, were too important to be lost. Many of these essential qualities were being ridiculed, undermined and commercialized. In the interest of the well-being of the nation the Government must act now. The proclamation called for the reform of the law concerning censorship so as to give the citizen freedom from offence and to stop the flagrant encouragement of abuses. Parents' rights regarding sex education in schools must be established. Broadcasting and films must be brought under effective control to ensure that they do not "offend against public feeling and decency", or, "incite to crime and disorder".

Bernard Madden, the young graphics designer who had produced some of the Festival's publicity material, came to the microphone to deliver what was together with that of Frank Deeks, the most impassioned speech of the rally addressed to the media. He challenged those present from the press and television to take careful note of the number of people present and to have proportionally representative reporting. "Why distort out of all proportion relatively minor events?" he asked. "Don't live in the media vacuum which so often creates its own values. Try to see more of the good that is in the world as it really is, and not just from the blinkered editorial desks of London." He called on editors, journalists, illustrators and photographers to act more responsibly in deciding what they should publish. "People matter more than scoops," he said. He castigated film and theatre producers for the all time high level of prolonged violence, blasphemy, sadism and perversion on stage and screen. The alternative press was urged to have a "real love based concern for man as man, not just as an animal". Aggression, hate, ridicule, bestiality, obscenity and depravity had no part in a loving concern to make a better society.

Following that, the proclamation to the media, read by David Kossoff, in his quiet, familiar voice, was something of a contrast. The media were criticised for too often attacking the positive values of love, family life, and respect for the dignity of the individual while violence, sex and irreverance were given quite undue prominence. As a powerful influence, the media had a responsibility to society and should therefore encourage productions which portrayed love and family life and the responsible use of freedom. They should also discourage the commercial exploitation of human perversion and weakness and ensure that their productions were not offensive or likely to incite to crime and disorder. Public issues must be dealt with fairly, and better means devised for considering complaints regarding broadcasting, films, the press and advertising.

George Goyder, prominent businessman and a member of the Church of England General Synod, read the proclamation to the Churches. It pointed out that many church members were among those gathering at Trafalgar Square and they affirmed the creation of man in God's image and his redemption through Jesus Christ. They shared with church leaders a sense of failure adequately to proclaim to the nation the dignity of man, which had been abused not only by environmental pollution and social injustice, but also by attacks on purity and family life and the commercial exploitation of sex and violence. The Churches had a major responsibility in taking a stand for positive Christian values against permissiveness and the proclamation therefore encouraged Church leaders to be publicly involved themselves in proclaiming Christian truth on moral questions, and in stimulating the involvement of all Christian people in moral debates.

All three proclamations were acclaimed virtually unanimously by the crowd, waving their summary sheets to indicate their assent, after which Peter Thompson, stressed to the crowd the part they could play individually in effecting a change in present trends. He urged them to seek an interview with their local Member of Parliament and ask him to press for action on sex films in schools which ignore parents' wishes, the setting up of a broadcasting council and a film council not appointed by the film industry but by competent members of the public. He urged individuals to approach their local councils and get them to set up special committees to look at X certificate films passed by the British Board of Film Censors with a view to refusing them a local licence. When there was an offensive advertisement or programme on TV they should write to the appropriate authority and complain.

By now time had more than run out and to close the proceedings the band struck up the National Anthem. "We knew it would upset a few people" said Eddie Stride afterwards, "but we also knew it would be approved by the majority." Some of those present in Trafalgar Square wondered whether too much was being packed into the programme, but the organizers were subsequently proved right in their judgement that, through the media, the eyes of the nation were focussed on the Square rather than the Park.

Throughout the proceedings even those who could hear what was being said from the platform were taking part in informal discussions with those in the crowd who opposed the Festival. Several of these became quite heated in their comments, but almost invariably they were spoken to in love and compassion. The major protest against the Festival elicited more sympathy than anger. About two-thirds of the way through the rally a procession entered the Square and marched along the pavement in front of the National Gallery. Led by a mock Christ carrying a cross they paraded round the Square with banners containing four letter words and other slogans bearing a casket labelled "Coffin of Liberty". They were preceded by some women chained together and dressed as, amongst other things, schoolgirls and young children. They made their way to the south side of the Square where the column and plinth are nearest to the road. A group of Festival supporters were round the back of the plinth out of earshot of the loudspeakers praying together for the rally.

By the time the protesters arrived the meeting was almost over and they gave a short demonstration of street theatre. Then as people started moving out of the square to form up for the march to Hyde Park the counter-demonstrators got hemmed in and jumped up on to the plinth to continue their demonstration. At a given signal the police moved in on the plinth and man-handled the demonstrators from their lofty perch. Some were brought to the ground and a struggle ensued before they were taken away in a police van. Several of the Festival of Light supporters who were watching the incident felt that the police had over-reacted to the situation, but is well to remember that there had been many threats about breaking up the rally and the police were obviously aiming to nip any such possibility in the bud.

Up at the north-west corner of the Square, quite unaware of what was going on within a couple of hundred yards of them, the first group of 2,000 marchers, including Mary Whitehouse and Malcolm Muggeridge, were sent on their way with the Salvation Army Band at the front followed by a huge wooden cross carried by several young men. While the rest of the crowd were waiting for their turn to join the march the Good News singers continued to play and there was other spontaneous singing.

There was a lot of singing on the march and great gaiety as the young people broke ranks and darted across the road to give tracts to passers by. Up Cockspur Street and into Arlington Street the marchers went, turning left into Piccadilly and thence to Hyde Park Corner. At one point the march passed right by a street newspaper seller who was effectively marooned from his potential customers by the endless stream of marchers. He seemed to take it all in good part and by the time the last of the marchers filed past him he had accumulated almost enough religious tracts and gospel leaflets handed to him by Festival supporters to start a religious bookshop.

Eddy Stride, who had a sprained ankle, went to Hyde Park by bus. As the bus overtook the marchers the sound of hymn-singing floated up the stairs to the top deck where he was sitting. His fellow passengers, he says, were visibly impressed. One American lady, on asking what it was all about, was told by another passenger that the people did not like nude magazines.

There was some delay for the marchers while they negotiated the heavily congested traffic roundabout at Hyde Park Corner and then they made their way up the north-bound carriage way of Park Lane towards Speaker's Corner. As they approached Marble Arch they were met by four to five hundred jeering demonstrators—more members of the Gay Liberation Front and Women's Liberation Movement who had been in evidence in Trafalgar Square. There were also anarchists and Communists, lined up against the railings of Hyde Park shouting "Sieg Heil" and throwing stink bombs and pieces of food at the marchers. As the band turned into the park and marched to the platform where the music festival was already in progress, the counter-demonstrators marched in front of them shouting and jeering.

As they flooded across the wide expanse of turf towards the site of the rally they came within earshot of the giant speakers poised on top of a mobile hydraulic crane sixty feet above the platform, over the top of which was the proud proclamation "Jesus Christ is the Solution". By the time they arrived in front of the platform the counter-demonstrators had been submerged in the growing crowd of marchers from Trafalgar Square who were now coming from the south having broken away from the main march at the gates to Hyde Park.

The music festival had started as planned at four o'clock with about 5,000 people present, some of whom had been diverted from the Square because it was full. Nigel Goodwin was the ebullient compère, keeping the audience on its toes with J-E-S-U-S shouts and Hallelujahs. Some of the marchers arrived in time to hear Cliff Richard sing. Terry Dene, Judy Mackenzie, Dana and Country Faith had all preceded Cliff, together with speakers Jean Darnall and Tony Sargent, and interviews with Ted Lyons and Alison Fraser-Skemp. The later part of the programme included the Forerunners, Graham Kendrick and Gordon Giltrap, together with speakers David MacInnes, David Watson and Arthur Blessitt. A collection for the Evangelical Alliance Relief Fund's work amongst the refugees in India, which realized nearly £1,700, was taken up.

David Watson addressed his remarks specifically to the Christians present. "If some people don't like us as Christians because, they say, we are always negative . . . maybe they are quite right, and we ourselves are at fault," he said. "I believe what Jesus is telling us here in Hyde Park is: 'Don't you just come to Hyde Park and tell the world to repent. Maybe you Christians also have to repent because: do *you* really love me? Do you really love other people?' " All too often, he said, people looked at Christians and saw neither the warmth of Jesus, nor his love. "Jesus is attractive, but we are not and our religious activities are not to those who don't share them. And I believe Jesus may well be saying, 'unless you repent; unless you come to love me as you ought to love me . . . I am going to take away your life altogether and instead of being a tremendous festival of light it will become a funeral of darkness, something which is utterly dead and utterly dreary.' "

As dusk fell the lights came on around the immediate area of the platform. The hot dog and Coca Cola stalls were doing a roaring trade particularly among the large number of people who were still arriving from the march. The crowd was in great good humour. There had been very few interruptions once the initial disturbance had died down, but there were plenty of animated conversations going on throughout the audience. Such banners as there were, seemed to belong to the Festival's opponents. One carried a quotation which read, "The streets of our country are in turmoil. The universities are filled with students rebelling and rioting. Communists are seeking to destroy our country. The country is in danger from within, and without law and order our nation cannot survive." The punchline was the person to whom the quote was attributed—Adolf Hitler in the year 1932.

By this time the programme was drawing to a close, but it was not finished before a memorable climax. With less than half an hour to go before the rally had to close Arthur Blessitt came on to the platform to give the final talk. All the activity in the park seemed to come to a halt as his distinctive voice boomed out over the loudspeakers. In vocal style, very reminiscent of Billy Graham, he made compulsive listening, as he drew together the threads of the afternoon's performance.

"We want all of England and the whole world to know that Jesus Christ is alive and real tonight," he said. "This is not a revolution that is soon to pass, just as it is not a revolution that has just begun. Our leader clearly is Jesus Christ. He is our Lord." He went on to say that the problems of war, hate, crime, lawlessness, drug addiction, alcoholism, and pornography were only outward symbols of a new spiritual emptiness. He spoke about his own conversion and his subsequent ministry, enlivening his talk with numerous stories from his own rich experience.

The audience loved it, but they were just as attentive when he challenged them to go out into the streets and subways and tell people about Jesus Christ, to go down into Soho and fill all the dirty books with Jesus tracts and to go and stand by the bookstalls and distribute Bibles.

Speaking of Christian discipleship he said that Jesus offered three things that nobody else would give—forgiveness of sins, purpose for living and His presence in a Christian's life. "Tonight could well be the most important night in modern history," he said, speaking specifically to Christians present. "You Christians, filled with the Holy Spirit, committed to Jesus Christ above all else, anchored in the Word of God, going out, sharing Christ all over Great Britain, can shake this land and change the course of history in this country."

Then he called on the vast audience to kneel and pray to God that he would send revival to England and the whole world. He closed his prayer with a short act of commitment, and then crowned the evening with an inspired stroke of pure genius. In an uncertain voice he started to sing the Lord's Prayer in the well-known Mallotte setting. He had no accompaniment, his voice was not good, he seemed to have pitched it too low and the crowd responded very slowly. But then as the volume swelled and the great climax was reached with the words "For Thine be the Kingdom, the Power and the Glory" the whole scene somehow fitted into place—the Mayfair skyline merging with the darkness, the traffic roaring unceasingly down Park Lane, the nation's capital getting down to another night's pleasure, whilst there in the Park a very contemporary and typical crowd the size of a football stadium was singing timeless words of praise to God.

There was time for one more "Jesus shout": "Give me a J, Give me an E, Give me an S, Give me a U, Give me an S, what have you got? Who do you love? Who will you serve? JESUS!" Then in a few short purposeful sentences Nigel Goodwin told the young people to go back to their own localities and put into practice what they had learnt that evening. Country Faith came on stage to play the "closing voluntary" as the great crowd started to break up and move out across the park back to the realities of everyday life.

At least fifty people went to the compound behind the platform afterwards for counselling and there were many serious conversations taking place in the crowd as it dispersed.

Young volunteers with large plastic litter bags ran enthusiastically all over the park picking up every available scrap of paper—and even a few dead leaves—hoping that the Park Superintendent would find his precious acres in immaculate condition the following morning. As the crowds made their way to the coaches waiting for them in Park Lane or to the London terminal stations for their special trains home there was again much singing and J-E-S-U-S shouting. At Marble Arch Underground station 500 young people descended on the ticket office wanting a ticket. The booking clerk, unused to such heavy traffic at that time of night, had to go and get a fresh stock of tickets. When he returned another 1,000 young people had arrived. According to reliable information, before he issued his last ticket he had been led to Christ! Several underground trains from Marble Arch were filled almost exclusively with Festival supporters who joined in singing, much to the amazement of the other passengers.

At Euston Station members of the "Jesus Liberation Front" started singing, and at once attracted a crowd. They then produced a tape recorder on which they replayed a tape of Arthur Blessitt's talk. By this time about 100 people had gathered round, and the impromptu meeting continued for two hours, with singing, testimonies and personal witness. Both the stationmaster and the police paid them a fleeting visit and left quite satisfied with the proceedings. At Waterloo Station a man commented to one of the organizers of the group from Southampton, "The people here are staggered. They keep getting young people coming up to them and saying 'Do you know the Lord Jesus? He's great!' and similar phrases."

So the light, having come to London, and flared up in a glorious blaze, now fanned out through the country, touching the hearts and lives of many who had not guessed at its significance.

Part Two

Chapter Six

SHEDDING A LITTLE LIGHT

WAS THE "moral pollution" picture as black as the Festival of Light propaganda painted? Could it not be written off as a paranoid reaction by a group of people oppressed with sexual guilt? What are the facts? How has the situation in Great Britain changed during the past twenty years in relation to public attitudes to sexual morality?

In the early 1950's the nation was still recovering from the longer term effects of the Second World War. Literature, broadcasting and the arts were only just getting back into their stride. There were, surprisingly enough, very much the same sort of restrictions upon what was permissible in the public sense as there are today, except for theatre censorship. But in those days the firmer grasp of traditional, if not Christian, values was reflected both in the lack of public demand for explicit sex and to a lesser extent violence, and in the degree of responsibility exercised by those who controlled the mass media.

Twenty years ago paperbacks were a virtual novelty and most books on the shelves were as sober in their jacket designs as they were in their contents. Such books as *Tropic of Cancer* and *Lady Chatterley's Lover* were available only on the black market, English editions printed overseas and smuggled into the country. Copies of Hank Janson novelettes, much thumbed and earmarked, were circulated surreptitiously among adolescents. What is generally called hard-core pornography was available in grubby back street shops in Soho and similar areas of other large cities but the demand for the services they offered was sufficiently meagre to dissuade more than a handful from setting up business in this way. The nation's bookstalls had nothing much more enticing than *Esquire* and *Man*, which boasted a few artistically posed models in glamorous attire or non-attire, and the ubiquitous *Health and Efficiency* together with other naturist magazines containing their regular quota of romping nudes suitably retouched. The press was largely on the side of traditional moral values, except for certain Sunday newspapers, who, as now, treated their readers to fully detailed accounts of the sexual adventures of high society and low life.

Films were, as now, subject to the dictates of the British Board of Film Censors who reacted sharply to anything more stimulating than a passionate kiss or embrace. Bedroom scenes were implied rather than visualized and violence was rarely if ever shown in all its gory detail.

The Lord Chamberlain kept a careful eye on the live theatre under powers granted to him as long ago as 1843. He required the submission of "the full dialogue and description of the action in any play for public performance and disallowed what in his opinion was immoral, obscene or indecent." But his jurisdiction did not cover music hall entertainment, which was subject only to the bylaws of the county council in which the performance took place. This loophole enabled some of the more adventurous impresarios to tour the country with musical shows and reviews incorporating a limited amount of nudity. So far as the Lord Chamberlain was concerned "A nude was rude if it moved", though he appeared to turn a paternalistically blind eye to the performances at London's famed Windmill Theatre, which as a result regularly drew a dominantly male audience to its continuous *Revaudeville* performances year in year out.

The BBC had a monopoly of all forms of broadcasting, with television still in its infancy and before the advent of the commercial channel. It took considerably more trouble then than would now appear to be the case to see that no programme transmitted "offended against good taste and decency or gave offence to public feeling or incited to crime and disorder". The influence of Lord Reith, the "father" of the BBC was still a powerful factor in programming.

In the field of advertising nothing like the slick professionalism which predominates today was evident, and such use of sex as was legitimately allowable in, for instance, posters advertising women's underwear, were generally kept below ground level on the escalators which served London's Underground railway system.

Sex education was very much the prerogative of the parents, and there was little instruction other than that of a specifically biological nature for children—and then not until mid-secondary school level. Books on the subject were written with moral fervour and sex education films were definitely a thing of the future.

That was the situation twenty years ago. What is it like now? What differences would a person notice returning to Britain after an absence of twenty years? And how have they taken place?

The world of literature can be said to have taken a dramatic turn in the direction on which it is now headed as a result of the successful publication by Penguin Books of D. H. Lawrence's *Lady Chatterley's Lover* in 1960. Seen in retrospect most people would agree that the book should not have been banned, but it is a fact of life that the unsuccessful prosecution brought against it by the Director of Public Prosecutions was the biggest single factor in releasing publishers from the sexual strait-jacket which had largely determined the extent of their publishing programme in this field up until that time.

The basis on which *Lady Chatterley's Lover* was cleared for publication was that it did not contravene the Obscene Publications Act of 1959 which states that "an article is deemed to be obscene if its effect is, if taken as a whole, such as to tend to deprave and corrupt persons who are likely, having regard to all the relevant circumstances, to read, see or hear the matter contained or embodied in it". Artistic and literary merit was held to be strong enough in this case for its sexual passages to pass unmolested. It is no exaggeration to say that only a very small proportion of books published since then about which publishers might have had second thoughts before the trial have made any claim to possess such literary and artistic merit.

The revolution in paperback publishing, with the cheap prices resulting from the streamlining of production costs and highly commercialized marketing methods has created a demand for books which glory in highly detailed erotica and sickening brutality. In a recent six million plus best-seller, *The Godfather* (to quote Richard Neville in *The Guardian*) "one of the book's more heroic figures culminates his criminal apprenticeship by binding up two men, stuffing towels in their throats to stifle screams, then with an axe methodically chopping off a pair of legs at the ankles, then at the knees, then at the thighs and so on, all of which should draw the crowds at the forthcoming movie. In real life such action would earn its perpetrator a prison sentence, but its fulsome depiction tumbles from bookstalls all over the world."

Another American book which sold two and a half million copies in the first two years was *Naked Came the Stranger*, which related in graphic detail the sexual adventures of an unfaithful wife with thirteen men. Its supposed young authoress Penelope Ashe was in fact a symposium of American journalists each of whom had written a chapter without reference to the others. It was a joke and yet an unabashed attempt to titillate the voyeurist instincts of its readers in a cynical, purely commercial way.

Despite the availability in general bookshops of so much material exploiting sex and violence (or perhaps because of it) the hard core pornography business is still booming. The traditional centre of pornographic bookshops in Britain is the Soho area of London. On a recent count there were found to be as many as between fifty and sixty shops operating in this field, and though no figures are available to enable a direct comparison to be made it can safely be said that there are far more now than was the case twenty years or even five years ago. They sell photographs, magazines, films, cartoons and cheaply produced duplicated books of crude sexual adventures, graphically overwritten and containing heterosexual and homosexual activity, flagellation, group sex, sadism, bestiality and all manner of perversions according to taste. Prices are high, starting at £3 to as much as £25 for a blue film. The main difference between the situation now and what it was twenty years ago is that with the freeing of restrictions on pornography in Denmark there is a much greater variety of material professionally produced than was the case before.

A growing number of publishers are producing pornographic books for distribution through mail order businesses. They solicit orders by sending illustrated brochures through the post to addresses which they have gained quite legally by access to the electoral rolls in a given district. Many of those receiving the brochures find them offensive, and in some cases harmful. Recent legislation has improved the situation but the abuse continues.

To the casual observer the world of men's magazines may not seemed to have changed much over the past twenty years. A few more titles, perhaps, more nudes on the front covers, but basically the same recipe as before. Nothing could be further from the truth. The old style men's magazines, *Blighty*, or *Parade* as it became, *Men Only* and others adopted what can best be described as a "saucy" attitude to sex, rather along the lines of the well-known seaside postcards. They had the pin-ups and the after dinner stories but their general attitude to sex was a lighthearted if vulgar one. Nude photography was very much regarded as an art form and glossy magazines specializing in it observed certain proprieties, namely, the model would never look directly at the camera, nor was her name mentioned.

The new-style sex magazines are in quite a different category. (And if it appears that a disproportionate amount of space is given to them here by comparison with other examples it must be realized that this type of pornography is the most readily available of all—40,000 newsagents' shops throughout the country stock at least some of this material —and it is available to anyone who wants it, however young. A boy of thirteen can buy a magazine containing pictures of scenes which have been censored out of X films he is not allowed to see.) By way of illustration *Men Only* can serve as an example. During the past few years it has undergone several changes in order to compete with others in the field. The arrival of *Playboy* in 1953 and its British equivalent *Penthouse* ten years later had begun the revolution in men's magazines. Both magazines and their subsequent imitators, urged their readers to indulge in their sexual appetites to the full without restriction. This was as much their right as it was to drive a car or play a round of golf. Erotic fantasy was to be encouraged and both magazines provided pictorial and written material to support this philosophy. There was a continual leap-frogging competition between them, each seeking to go one better.

The whole market was shattered in the summer of 1971 when Paul Raymond, a strip club and nude theatre impresario, bought the ailing *Men Only* and another equally ailing magazine *Escort*, merging them under the former title and relaunching them in the now accepted format of *Penthouse* and the others. He threw overboard virtually all the existing conventions to which his competitors paid lip service and portrayed more nudes per square inch, complete with pubic hair, and more explicit descriptions per column inch than any of his rivals had ever dared print. W. H. Smith's immediately refused to stock the magazine, though they continued distribution to wholesalers until February 1972, but its circulation has leapt up by an incredible 700 per cent in six months, from a meagre 35,000 to reportedly over a quarter of a million. Much of the material in the issue current at the time of writing is precisely that which could have landed any bookseller stocking it five years ago in jail.

The "glamour" photographs are aggressively erotic, concentrating on the genital area to an almost obsessive degree. The fiction consists mainly of erotic fantasies incorporating sexual deviations, perversions, cruelties, sadism, and in general sex of the rawest type. The two words that are never mentioned are love and marriage. There is much pseudo-scientific "sexological" writing which purports to reproduce in every minute detail the sexual experiences of those who contribute. (This style reached its nadir with the revelations in *Men Only* of a woman who allegedly toured Europe having sexual relations with men of each nationality and reported back in purple prose her own intimate and detailed version of the incidents and her reactions.) This type of writing can be masked with the solemn cloak of scientific investigation, or find a home in the correspondence columns, but it contains all the hallmarks of pornographic fantasy. The whole aim seems to be to emphasize brute sexuality at the expense of sensitive feelings.

That these magazines are reaching an increasing public is shown by the fact that two of the "softer" men's magazines, *Parade* and *Carnival*, whose combined sales per issue totalled 380,000 copies in 1967, sold only 134,000 per issue in the first half of 1970, whilst the combined circulations of *Penthouse* and *Mayfair*, its chief rival until *Men Only* was revived, have increased in the same period from 246,000 to 382,000 copies per issue. In the middle of 1971 City Magazines Ltd., publishers of *Carnival* and *Parade*, were taken over by Rupert Murdoch, of the *News of the World*. Since then they have developed something of the combination of aggressive sexuality and explicitness as the other magazines. It is too early yet to say if this development has changed their circulation trend. A further indication of the failure of the non-aggressive approach was marked by the closure of *Club* early in 1972.

The men's magazines make no false claims for themselves. They are for "entertainment". There is another category of sex magazines which if they could be taken seriously should be termed "educational". The first of these, *Forum*, was pioneered by the publishers of *Penthouse* in 1967. It takes the pseudo-scientific section of its parent magazine to its ultimate conclusion. Eschewing the glossy full-colour nudes it has a small page size with unadorned typography and concentrates exclusively on "psycho-sexual" matters, encouraging full and frank discussion in its correspondence columns of sexual guilt, deviancy, incredible feats of sexual athleticism, every possible variation of sexual intimacy, and so on.

This type of magazine (there are half a dozen different titles on the market now) has led in turn to a rash of big colourful illustrated magazines combining the sex educational stance of the smaller variety with pictures which only a few months ago would have relegated them to the back room of the Soho bookshops—full frontal nudes, male and female, romping around, simulating intercourse and other fantasy experiences. It is almost impossible to take the declared "educational" intentions of these magazines seriously, the writing so bizarre and the pictures so obviously titillating. The bookstalls certainly don't—displaying them alongside all the other "girlie" magazines, generally near the cash desk to discourage furtive peeps at the contents by undecided purchasers or bookshop voyeurs.

A fourth category of sex magazines is that which revolves around the cinema. The traditional movie magazines have always had their share of X film pictures but these new magazines concentrate exclusively on virtually uncensored films, i.e., those which are shown on the rapidly growing cinema club circuits. They can only be as explicit as the films which they are featuring, though it is very often the case that stills from a film shown in the magazines are not subsequently a part of the actual film.

There remain two further types of sex magazine which are some way from being hard-core pornography. The imported American girlie and personal revelations magazines have long been a feature of newsagents in most large towns. They are garish, shoddy, anonymous productions which often promise more on the front cover than they actually reveal inside. They are probably what the average person thinks of when the phrase "girlie magazines" is mentioned. But in fact there is all the difference in the world between the random selection of an almost indistinguishable and certainly anonymous American magazine and the regular purchase of a proudly identifiable, legitimate British one, such as those mentioned earlier. The last type of sex magazine is that which would probably classify itself as pseudo-pornography. British produced, they contain either picture strip versions of sexual fantasies or sequences of lesbian or "kinky" sexual activity. They are generally cellophane-wrapped to prevent prior perusal of the contents and are artificially highly priced to give the purchaser a false impression as to the daring nature of what he is buying.

It is very difficult to say how many of these sex magazines are in circulation. Many of them are undated and newsagents simply restock their shelves with different varieties. Of those published monthly only the men's entertainment magazines publish verifiable circulation figures to attract advertising—and also to score off their competitors! From these it is clear that at the time of writing the total sale of the eight men's entertainment magazines is somewhere in the region of a million copies a month—at 30p to 40p a time. The so-called "educational" and X cinema magazines, around a dozen in all, may well sell a further half million copies a month—at 40p to 50p a time. Nobody knows just how many American girlie and pseudo-pornographic magazines are sold (though the annual turnover of just one British producer of the latter type is £500,000), but discounting these we are already talking of a total circulation in excess of the British edition of the *Readers' Digest*.

With the obvious exception of the American girlie magazines most of these magazines are printed and published in this country. The men's entertainment magazines carry advertisements for liquor, cigars, watches and other commodities marketed by reputable British firms. Both they and the "educational" magazines run bookclubs offering what are virtually pornographic books to their readers at special prices. Many of the magazines are handled by commercial wholesalers who are responsible for the large scale movement of all periodicals and newspapers. Indeed one of them was published by that bastion of respectability the International Publishing Corporation. As has already been mentioned the major selling outlets are the 40,000 local newsagents, but they are also widely sold by street newspaper sellers. Of the two major retail newsagent's chains, W. H. Smiths are rather more selective in what they stock. John Menzies appear to follow a policy of "anything goes". In other words, this whole field of sex magazine publishing has been "legitimatized" in a way which five years ago would have barely seemed credible.

By their very nature newspapers are not in the pornographic business in a direct sense, but they can be pacesetters in changing social attitudes to public morality. No one man has done more in this context than Rupert Murdoch whose arrival on the British newspaper scene was the biggest event in Fleet Street since Lord Thomson's advent. Murdoch first acquired the *News of the World*, long an exponent of the call-girl exposé and seamy court case type of journalism. He did little to change the pattern, merely improving the formula, though he did make a notable contribution to the paper's accumulated bad taste when he authorized the republication of the sordid details of a well-known political scandal of the early 1960's.

Not satisfied with the acquisition of the nation's biggest selling Sunday newspaper he went on to purchase the *Sun*, which was at that time an ailing broadsheet, seeking to uphold, without much success, the aims and outlook of the Trades Union Movement. He revamped it into a direct copy of the *Daily Mirror* and started out on an incredibly successful publishing venture which still shows no signs of tailing off. In the two years since he took it over the circulation rose from 850,000 to around 2½ million copies a day, but to achieve this Murdoch concentrated heavily on sex, including serializations of several books with that as their theme, numerous sex surveys and the inevitable smattering of topless and occasionally bottomless girls. To look at an average issue of the *Sun*, or some of its rivals now, since they were forced to copy Murdoch's tactics to a degree to keep level in the circulation stakes, it is difficult to believe that the first topless picture of a girl to appear in a British newspaper to the accompaniment of a considerable furore was only six years ago.

Recent years have seen the growth of an "underground" press running parallel to the "straight" or overground press. Any analysis of these papers is made difficult by their sheer variety and number. The best known, since the trial of its editors, is probably *Oz*, but others which have achieved a certain notoriety include *International Times*, *Black Dwarf* and *Frendz*. These papers are produced on shoestring budgets, mainly by highly committed young people, many of anarchist persuasion, and seek to propagate the concept of an alternative society. They are unconventional both in their style, content and layout, and use visual imagery, particularly sexual imagery, to get across many of their points.

The producers of the underground papers cannot really be identified with the capitalist pornographers behind the glossy magazines for they are self-evidently poor in this world's goods and are committed to an idealogical point of view which however much one may disagree with is more commendable than the commercial motives of the get-rich-quick pornographers. Whatever their motives, however, the editors of the underground press, by their concentration on sexual matters have helped to identify their publications in the eyes of the public—and certainly the newsagents—with the material we have already discussed. And whilst the underground press is not specifically aimed at children and young people it is clear that copies of these papers are much more likely to come into the hands of young people than the glossy type of magazine, and because of the nature of their general content are more likely to commend themselves to the younger generation. Viewed in isolation the sexual material contained in much of the underground is grotesquely obscene, as the *Oz* trial made clear.

Mention has already been made of the increasingly explicit sexual content of films. The British Board of Film Censors is still the governing body so far as film censorship is concerned, though they now have an additional category, AA, in which to place films that fall somewhere between the old X and A categories. Nudity on the screen first became acceptable in the late 1950's when naturist films were all the rage and nudity in the natural surroundings of the nudist camp was suddenly seized upon as a commercial goldmine. Despite the steadying influence of the censor it was only a matter of time before nudity infiltrated the rest of the film world. Now it is scarcely possible to go and see anything other than a U film which does not contain nudity of some sort, and often sexually explicit love scenes.

Films such as these, which go on general release, are not

always the big money-spinners. There is a circuit of cinemas in London and all the big cities which show a continuous diet of "Xey Sexies", many of them running for several months and nearly all of them low budget productions by small companies. These may either be straightforward narrative films or supposedly sex education films such as "Anatomy of Love" which ran at a small cinema in London for almost a year. A glance at the Entertainments Guide of a London evening paper provides sufficient evidence of the large number of films in this category.

Not content with the freedom thus allowed in London's smaller cinemas, Kenneth Rive, a continental film distributor, runs a chain of cinema clubs in London and the major cities to show films which are far more explicit than the X films already mentioned. Because the audiences at these clubs are technically members they are able to see films over which the authorities have no control. His original declared intention was thus to allow responsible and mature adults to see artistic films which the "bigoted and narrow minded censor" would not allow them to see. In point of fact the films, nearly all of which are banal and poorly made, are screened to the regular voyeuristic trade usually caricatured as "the raincoat men" but which now in fact includes those from the whole social spectrum. One chain of cinema clubs has thirty five cinemas in its group with 130,000 members. All that is necessary is for one print of a film to be purchased and shown at each cinema in rotation, thus cutting down overheads and providing rich rewards for the promoters.

The activities of these fringe cinema operators is naturally having its effect on the big-time commercial cinema and in an effort to win back some of the lost audiences (attendances of thirty-one million a week in 1949 have dropped to around six million) two films were produced by major American studios and sent on general release early in 1971. *Beyond the Valley of the Dolls* and *Myra Breckenridge* were panned by the critics and in fact did not succeed at the box office, but they brought the general level of commercial general release films to a new low with nudity, drug taking, and sexual perversions in abundance. An earlier film, *Secrets of Sex*, had an overtly sadistic storyline in which conflict and hatred between the sexes was constantly emphasized—at one point the horrific picture of a deformed baby in an incubator was used by way of illustrating the theme. These and other similar films were put in the shade, however, by Ken Russell's film *The Devils* which received an equally adverse reception from the critics but has since become a major box office success. The film, which tells the story of a seventeenth century priest in France and his clash with the establishment, includes scenes of torture and brutality as well as explicit sexual activity between the nuns.

This in turn has been superceded by *Straw Dogs*, which according to one critic "makes *The Devils* seem like a vicarage tea party". Alexander Walker, film critic of the London *Evening Standard*, had this to say: "What the film censor has permitted on the screen in *Straw Dogs* makes one wonder whether he has any further useful role to play in the cinema industry. To have made such a vicious and degrading film appears an aberration of judgement on someone's part. To pass it on for public exhibition in its present form is tantamount to a dereliction of duty. For if this goes, then anything goes." The film combines sex and violence in a way which, he says, "appears to cater for those possessed of the instinctual frenzy of a glutton's appetite." In a joint letter with twelve other leading film critics Walker wrote to *The Times* deploring the film.

Long before the commercial cinema was hit by these permissive trends substandard gauge films circulating amongst amateurs were "revealing all". For several years a large variety of glamour films have been stridently advertised in the photographic trade press. Harmless fantasies though many of them may seem, the cumulative effect of this massive exposure of the female form has been another factor in this developing situation.

The theatre was not slow to test its new found freedom following the abolition of the Lord Chamberlain's censorship powers in 1967. Since then London's West End has seen the work of Edward Bond and his Theatre of Cruelty, *Council of Love* (described by one critic as "breathtakingly blasphemous"), the sex comedies presented by Paul Raymond and the two London shows current at the time of writing *Oh Calcutta!* and *The Dirtiest Show in Town*, both of which have been described by their backers as elegant pornography and contain nudity and simulated intercourse amongst other sexual antics. In the case of these latter shows actors and actresses had become physically ill by taking part in the shows while others have only appeared in them because the alternative would be unemployment. It is also clear that however high minded the intention of the originators of the shows may have been in the context of intellectual sophistication they are mainly attracting the curious coachloads up from the provinces.

Music hall entertainment is now virtually a thing of the past. It if has a present day equivalent it must be the strip clubs which have proliferated in London and the major cities during the past ten years. The idea behind them came from a restaurant owner in London in the late 1950's who discovered that by the simple expedient of opening a theatre club he was able to produce intimate revues completely outside the Lord Chamberlain's control. The idea quickly caught on and the number of such clubs has now grown from around half a dozen ten years ago the to present figure of between fifty and sixty in London alone. The façade of a technical membership fee and waiting period before admittance has long since been waived and the shows are completely open to the public. The romantic notion widely perpetuated that the performances are inoffensive if not boring is singularly wide of the mark. Increasing genital display and lesbian couplings of a type not far short of the Danish "live shows" are very much the order of the day.

Literature, the cinema and the theatre are all indulged in as a matter of positive choice. The broadcasting media are in a different category, being virtually on tap directly within the home. In so far as television and radio have mirrored developments in the arts and literature they have of necessity included increasingly in their programmes material which emphasizes sexual infidelity and lust together with the gratuitous use of violence. It is in the field of television drama where the all-pervading permissiveness is mostly evident, with plays emphasizing infidelity in marriage, promiscuity and sexual deviancy outside it, and virtually writing off traditional standards of sexual morality. There have been growing fears about the amount of violence on the television screens, particularly an ITV Series *Big Breadwinner Hog* in 1969.

A wave of cynicism and irreverent satire begun with *That was The Week That Was* in 1963 and continued in similar programmes, was the prelude to a period when under a very liberal-minded director-general "a fall occurred in BBC standards which unfortunately is still continuing", to quote John Stokes MP writing to *The Times*. There was some correspondence in the *Daily Telegraph* in the Autumn of 1971 concerning the charge that there was a general bias in television, during the course of which both David Holbrook, the writer, and Malcom Muggeridge, accused the broadcasting media of "unfairness, impertinence and bias" concerning those "opposed to the prevalent dogmas of permissiveness." There has been much public agitation in this field over the past eight years as a result of the work of Mrs. Mary Whitehouse, whose Clean-up TV Campaign and subsequent National Viewers and Listeners Association has attracted much support from the British public and it must be added, a measure of scorn.

Sex education for children has mushroomed during the past twenty years. Whilst most rational people welcome the open and frank discussion of sexual matters which has been a feature of recent years more recently there have been some disquieting developments. The schools radio programme *Learning about Life* intended for the fourteen to sixteen age group, has, amongst other things, advocated the practice of masturbation as a preparation or rehearsal for sexual intercourse, taken a virtually amoral attitude to homosexuality and sexual intercourse outside marriage, and implied that responsibility in sexual relations between the partners was simply a matter of considering each other's sexual needs and choosing an effective contraceptive.

During 1971 a sex education film entitled *Growing Up* was shown by Dr. Martin Cole of Birmingham, which contained film of masturbation and also full sexual intercourse, together with a commentary which completely divorced the subject from any moral considerations.

The same can be said for *The Little Red Schoolbook* which was published in 1971 and was the subject of a court case for obscenity. In a section on sex intended for young people in the fourteen to sixteen age group it attacks existing standards of sexual morality, advocates contraceptive machines in schools, together with the fullest sexual experimentation between boys and girls, including the use of pornographic material if it is helpful. Veneral disease is played down and abortion treated as every girl's right. In fairness to the book it must be said that it contains what is probably the best argued case against smoking and drugs currently available for young people, but the book was rightly judged obscene in the courts, though an expurgated version has now been published which makes only minimal alterations to the text. The book originated in Denmark and was translated into English for marketing here.

A sex education hand-book for teachers issued by Exeter Education Authority entitled *Scheme of Education in Personal Relationships* states that "all relationships between people of the same sex are homosexual" (dictionary definition: having a sexual propensity for persons of one's own sex), and claims that these relationships can be beneficial in early life. A father of two children at the school who kept them at home as a protest against the book was subsequently fined. He has now moved them to another school.

The advertising world has been slower than many people anticipated in exploiting the selling potential of sex, but increasingly nudity or near nudity and sexual innuendo is used to sell a large variety of goods and products, both on large advertisement hoardings, in special promotions, press advertisements and through the intimacy of television commercials. The 1971 Motor Show was marked for the first time by the appearance of nude girls to promote new models, a fertilizer corporation invested in a huge full-page nude in

The Times newspaper and a cigar manufacturer provided a short erotic fantasy in a TV commercial entirely unrelated to his product, except that they both give pleasure to a man.

The extent to which what has been mentioned in this chapter is obscene in the terms of the 1959 Obscene Publications Act is a matter for some speculation. Whether it is or is not, most of it is pornographic in the sense that it exploits depersonalized sex for commercial or ideological gain and is also likely to lead to a coarse animalistic attitude to sexual relationships. The stakes in the pornography business are high. There are many fortunes to be made and as each barrier is overrun, as each convention is discarded, so inevitably pornographic material will move away from "straight" sex to deviations, perversions, sadism, violence and cruelty, with incalculable results.

This is not just scaremongering talk. It is already happening in some of the highly competitive areas that have been discussed. And while the chief cause for concern may well be the mass media of press, radio and television, what happens in the theatre, the cinema and literature inevitably has an increasingly significant effect upon the more popular mass media. Children growing up today may well have a much more open and uninhibited attitude to sexuality, which will be all to the good, but they are nevertheless being exposed to material freely available as it is through many outlets, which no one has yet clearly shown could not cause grave damage to their developing attitudes towards sex.

Chapter Seven

IN A BAD LIGHT

The media coverage of the Nationwide Festival of Light was probably the biggest for any specifically religious event since the Papal Encyclical on Birth Control in 1968. By the middle of October the number of press cuttings received at the Festival headquarters was nearing the 750 mark and the number of people who had seen, heard or read about the festival throughout the world was conservatively estimated at 600 million. Obviously the way the media handled their coverage is as vital in assessing the long term impact of the Festival.

As has already been suggested, there was at the start some antipathy toward the Festival on the part of press, quite naturally, because the media in general were among those castigated by its propaganda. An added barrier was probably the rather defensive attitude adopted by the Festival organizers to the press, both at national and regional levels.

But having made all due allowances over these factors the media coverage of the Festival of Light left much to be desired, certainly in terms of the national press and broadcasting media.

The original press announcement was, as we have already noticed, in the form of a freelance journalist's story. By and large the papers printed the story as they were given it, though most of them emphasized its anti-porn rather than its pro-family life aspects. The provincial press who on these matters are generally serviced by the Press Association, were generally more positive in their treatment of it though somewhat attenuated.

The provincial press continued to feature the Festival as they received information from local organizers and the national press carried the occasional story referring to it. But it was not until Peter Thompson came on the scene in mid-August with a planned public relations programme for the Festival that there was any attempt to utilize the media in a cohesive and effective way.

Thompson felt that he had inherited what the media saw as virtually a Muggeridge/Whitehouse/Longford anti-porn crusade and his first move was to try to emphasize the young people involved in the project. His first notable success was in the *Daily Express* of August 31 when there was a well documented feature in which Ruth Mason, one of the secretaries, and Peter Hill were given the major coverage and Dora Bryan, Cliff Richard and David Kossoff were relegated to the middle of the article. Whitehouse, Muggeridge and Longford were not mentioned. But this was the only occasion on which the press took that line. From then until after the Festival itself it was definitely Muggeridge, Whitehouse and Longford, all the way.

The first major encounter with the press came on September 9, the day of the inaugural rally and press conference. What happened at the press conference has already been covered in some detail in an earlier chapter. The events of that evening pushed into the background some of the things said at the press conference but it is still instructive to analyse the reports in the early editions of the national papers and the original story circulated by the Press Association to the provincial papers. The London *Times* in a piece headlined "Promotion of Moral Pollution a 'fraud backed by intelligensia' ", covered the press conference in about six inches, referring to Peter Hill's original vision and announcement of the plans for the Festival. The remainder was a write up in advance of the evening rally culled from advance handouts of the two main speeches by Malcolm Muggeridge and Bishop Huddleston. No mention was made in *The Times* of the communications between Col. Dobbie and Dr. Ramsey, Archbishop of Canterbury. For all the other papers it was the main point of the whole exercise until it was superceded by the bogus nuns.

More than half the *Telegraph's* ten inch report was devoted to the exchange of words between Col. Dobbie and John Miles, the Archbishop's press officer, with nothing more than the briefest summary of what Peter Hill, Malcolm Muggeridge, Johnny Noer and Trevor Huddleston, had to say. The *Guardian* had the most substantial coverage of the press conference of all the national dailies, though written with its characteristic whimsy, it gave good coverage to Malcolm Muggeridge and Bishop Huddleston, together with comments from Peter Hill and Steve Stevens, a small extract from the appendix to the Festival's Statement of Intent and a short paragraph about the Archbishop's attitude to the Festival which, alone among the national dailies, put the matter in the right perspective.

The Press Association sent out two stories, one a summary of Malcom Muggeridge's address at the Central Hall, much of which, as it turned out, he did not deliver, and a write up of the morning press conference which concentrated exclusively on the Archbishop's "blessing" or lack of it.

And that would have been the sum total as far as the press was concerned had it not been for the interruptions and disturbances at the meeting because of Operation Rupert. Only the *Guardian* and *The Times* were represented at the inaugural rally itself, together with a reporter and photographer from the Press Association, and they were probably beginning to think they were wasting their time when it suddenly became alive with the organized demonstration and the bogus nuns (a gift to any press reporter) who "ran howling" (*Guardian*) "cavorted" (*The Times*) "charged" (*Press Association*) the platform. The two men phoned their stories through to their papers, and there was much rejigging of pages.

The Times slotted the protest story on top of the existing Festival story, changed the headline to "Uproar at Central Hall as Demonstrators Threaten to Halt the Festival of Light" and added a couple of Press Association pictures of a demonstrator and Muggeridge. The *Guardian*'s man wrote a complete story concentrating on the disturbance, which was printed in the paper's later editions together with the same two Press Association photos, replacing John Windsor's very fair write up of the press conference carried in the paper's earlier editions. The Press Association's man telephoned his story through to the newsdesk in Fleet Street and it went straight out on the tapes to be picked up by several of the national papers and most of the provincial papers in their later editions. The Press Association story reported the disturbance, together with three paragraphs referring to the earlier press conference, exclusively dealing with the alleged refusal of Dr. Ramsey to give the Festival his blessing.

The *Telegraph* picked up the PA story and put in an abbreviated version on its front page, subsequently rejigging its original story and cutting the whole thing down to about six inches concentrating on the demonstration and the Archbishop's "blessing". The *Sun*, the *Daily Mirror* and the *Daily Express* all carried the later Press Association story, suitably rewritten which rather suggests that had there not been the counter-demonstration no mention of the Festival would have been made in their pages at all. Thus a movement claiming the potential support of over 100,000 people throughout the country, and launched in London with a rally attracting in excess of 4,000 was dismissed in half a dozen paragraphs dealing with a small minority demonstration at the rally and a trivial misunderstanding over Dr. Ramsey's "blessing". With one or two honourable exceptions, no reference was made to the real aims and intentions of the Festival nor was any space devoted to the representations of the Danish speakers who claimed to present a different picture of Denmark's pornographic freedom than that which is usually painted. (The *Slough Evening Mail* is a very honourable exception in that respect; they printed one of the Danish press releases in full.)

Perhaps realizing that the reporting of the rally could hardly have been described as balanced, both the *Guardian* and the *Sunday Times* carried leading articles at the weekend criticizing the anti-demonstrators at the rally for not allowing the Festival organizers the freedom to hold their meeting in peace. "In traditional style, an anti-repressive movement thus announces itself by seeking to repress a gathering of people the very first time these people show a capacity to organize themselves against cultural trends of which, quite legitimately, they disapprove." (*Sunday Times*) "It ill behoves those who themselves demand tolerance and understanding to offer so little to the Bishop and his fellows." (*Guardian*)

After the storm came the lull, so far as the national press was concerned, but the provincial and local papers carried on the debate about the Festival in their correspondence columns and printed feature articles and news reports of local plans for rallies and beacons. The national press had its difficulties throughout this period with distribution problems and union discontent which affected several of the papers during the run-up period to the Festival. There were no national papers at all on the Thursday of the beacon lighting, and coverage in the following day's newspapers was understandably sketchy in view of the pressure of other news which had accumulated during the break in publication.

As already mentioned in an earlier chapter, hoax letters were sent out by opposition groups to some regional organizers telling them to avoid Trafalgar Square and go straight to Hyde Park. This was, of course, a gift so far as last minute publicity for the Festival was concerned. The story was given to the Press Association who spread it around very widely, but due to the difficulties in the national press it only appeared in an abbreviated form in *The Times*, the *Guardian* and the *Sun*. The provincial press, however, not having the problems which Fleet Street was experiencing, used the story extensively, some of them in full.

On the Saturday morning of the Trafalgar Square and Hyde Park rallies both London evening papers ran stories on the event, not unnaturally with an eye to potential sales. Rather strangely, in view of their respective cultural/sociological affinities, the *Evening Standard* came off much the better of the two, with a preparatory feature in its earlier editions, subsequently replaced by picture coverage and a short write up. By contrast the *Evening News* tucked the story away on an inside page with a write up occupying about one and a half inches, a picture not much bigger and the rather misleading headline "250,000 Mass for Anti-Porn Rally". No change was made in the headline or the story in the paper's later editions because it was on one of the pages which remained constant throughout the day.

There must have been a noticeable surge in sales of Sunday papers on the day following the Festival as many who perhaps did not normally buy a Sunday paper invested in one just to see what they said about the rallies. Depending upon which paper they bought they would have been satisfied, puzzled and thoroughly angry, for the press coverage ranged from the reasonably adequate to the thoroughly reprehensible. As far as can be ascertained, all seven of the English Sunday papers had reporters in Trafalgar Square, and to a lesser extent in Hyde Park together with a bevy of cameramen, which suggests an accurate assessment of the Festival's newsworthiness. The *Sunday Telegraph* and the *Observer* both gave front page, well illustrated coverage which revealed a fair, balanced and largely accurate view of the proceedings. The *Sunday Telegraph* straddled its back page with a remarkable three part picture taking in virtually the whole of the crowd in the Square. This was subsequently used on the Festival's 1971 Christmas card. They are, as it happens, the two Sunday papers with the smallest circulations, between them accounting for only six per cent of total Sunday sales of over 25 million.

The "big boys" handled the story quite differently, led rather surprisingly by the *Sunday Times*, which only two weeks earlier had carried a leading article emphasizing the right of the Festival supporters to a fair hearing of their case. Their story was headlined "Light Rally Clash: 27 arrests" and concentrated virtually all of its twelve inches on the activities of the handful of demonstrators from the Gay Liberation Front and elsewhere who had demonstrated during the closing stages of the rally. The meeting itself was dismissed in a single sentence, "Undoubtedly the 30,000 young people in Trafalgar Square reached a state of euphoria after the chants, hymns, the forest of arms pointing to God, and the demands for more censorship". The report was accompanied by two photographs which could not have been more unrepresentative of the crowd in the Square. Ignoring the large number of positive and happy banners that were displayed, their cameraman picked on what must have been the only three traditional banners of "The Wages of Sin is Death" variety in the whole Square.

In fairness to the *Sunday Times* it must be said that following representations to Harold Evans and Dennis Hamilton of the Times Organization by, amongst others, Peter Thompson, Malcolm Muggeridge and Lord Longford, some reparation was made the following week with a balanced article by William Shawcross about Peter Hill and the background to the Festival. A more truly representative photograph of the Festival was also published together with two letters of complaint at the previous week's coverage which were representative of such a large number that the editor had to have a special letter duplicated to cope with the problem of answering them all.

For some reason only two of the papers reported the message which Prince Charles sent to the rally, offering "every good wish for the success of the Festival". The *Sunday Mirror* made it its lead with a banner headline "Royal Swipe at Porn" and a picture of the Prince, together with a headline, "Anti-porn, Prince Charles Signs on with the Clean-Up Brigade", occupying a quarter of its front page. It was somewhat ironic that the remaining three-quarters of the page was occupied with pictures of naked couples embracing as a foretaste of its serialization of extracts from Desmond Morris's book *Intimacy*. Apart from its coverage of Prince Charles' good wishes and various reactions to his message, the report devoted most of its remaining space to descriptions of the underground protest, concluding with four short paragraphs summarizing the proclamations. Two large accompanying pictures concentrated exclusively on the counter-demonstrators and the tussle with the police.

The remaining three popular Sunday papers were substantially briefer in their coverage. *The People* led with Prince Charles' support of the Festival and gave approximately equal space to what was said at the rally and the counter-demonstration. The *Sunday Express* report carried the one headline which the organizers had prophesied would be bound to turn up somewhere in reports of the Hyde Park rally, "Smoke Bombs as Cliff Sings". It devoted two-thirds of its space to details of the protest at the Park and at Trafalgar Square. The *News of the World* parodied the whole thing, as a "Saints versus Sinners" confrontation, squeezing their four inch story on to the bottom of an inside page. Considering that typical headlines to some of their other stories were "Mother of Two and Boy of Fifteen Missing", "Scoutmaster Groom and Boy Vanish", "Britains Sexiest Girl Contest", "When No Nudes is Good News", "Husbands for Sale" and, inevitably, "She Fought for Her Honour in Pillbox", to say nothing of a feature on Stag Shows and a series on the British Way of Loving, it is not difficult to see which side the *News of the World* is on (and they say the Festival of Light is obsessed with sex!).

Several of Monday morning's papers made passing reference to the Festival, among them the *Morning Star*, which had chosen an admittedly extraordinary picture of a rather over-enthusiastic young man leading one of the J-E-S-U-S shouts with finger pointed to the sky. Under the headline "Festival of Light Harps Back to the Dark Ages", the report assured its readers that the picture was not Nuremburg in the Thirties but Trafalgar Square on the previous Saturday. "Resurrection of the dark ages of sexual suppression and guilt was apparently not the only target of a number of those in the highly organized and expensively equipped congregation," it read, claiming that those involved in the counter-protest were bombarded with shouts of "Kill a Commie for Christ" and that one banner carried by a marcher showed radiant swastikas. This report was taken to task later in the week by the Rev. Michael Scott, who at one time represented affairs of tribal chiefs in South West Africa at the United Nations General Assembly. He described it as a "most mischievous and scurrilous misrepresentation". He clearly felt that the comment and banner referred to came from members of the counter-demonstration though this was later challenged.

Both the *Daily Mail* and the *Daily Telegraph* had leading articles on the Festival, the *Mail* being cautiously in favour, the *Telegraph* being rather stuffily pedantic. The *Financial Times* dismissed the whole thing in a curt paragraph referring to fifteen people being charged with insulting behaviour during the Festival demonstration.

An incident took place during the week following the Festival which some felt emphasized that bias in the press about which the Festival was protesting in its proclamation to the media. On Tuesday September 28 Mr. Kenneth Furness, general secretary of the British Humanist Association, issued a statement criticizing Prince Charles for "lending his support" to the Festival. The paid-up membership of the BHA is less than 3,000 and yet the statement received ten times more publicity in the papers the following day than did the Prince's original message—which had been given to a crowd of 35,000. (Ironically, this particular publicity gambit by the BHA rather backfired. Had they not issued a statement criticizing the Prince's action the great British public would probably have been quite unaware that he had ever sent his best wishes "for the success of the Festival", since that fact was only mentioned in two newpaper reports of the event whereas the BHA statement was reported—sometimes in full—in twenty or more.)

Several papers published articles in the immediate post-Festival period, giving some account of how it built up and emphasizing (at last!) the part played throughout by young people. It is hard to say whether this was a case of jumping on the bandwagon, redressing the balance or giving in to Peter Thompson's blandishments. Probably it was a mixture of all three. The weekly reviews virtually ignored the Festival save for a few snide remarks here and there and a somewhat cautious piece in the *Economist:* "That kind of mass chanting and barely controlled hysteria (a reference to the Trafalgar Square rally) has never taken root in the majority in Britain. Dr. Billy Graham has come and gone and left the country looking much as before . . . The tone of last Saturday's Festival was on the whole constructive, not repressive, loving, not hating or envying . . . Those who supported the Festival are no doubt going to keep a strict eye on the activities of their fellow men. They themselves may need to be watched lest their original intentions degenerate into the kind of narrow rigorous persecution which has masqueraded as Christian example so often in the past."

The religious press, as was to be expected, contained the most extensive coverage of the Festival, and their attitude is summarized in a later chapter. The 1,500 or so local and provincial newspapers gave a large amount of space to the Festival as the six or seven volumes of press cuttings at Festival headquarters demonstrate.

So much for the press. How did the radio and television networks react to the Festival? This was Peter Thompson's particular forté and the area in which he had the most useful contacts. But, as Thompson wrote in a letter to the *Daily Telegraph*, "It is significant to note that while the television networks in this country were not prepared to document the Festival in television terms the American and Canadian television networks thought otherwise". He could have added that there were television reporters present also from Austria, Holland, Denmark, Sweden, Germany, Italy and France; radio reporters from Canada, Finland, Rumania, Czechoslovakia and Poland; and newsreel films distributed in seventy-two countries.

British radio bulletins and television newscasts gave adequate coverage of the Trafalgar Square and Hyde Park rallies, but a particular cause of anger among the Festival organizers was the report, if such it can be called, broadcast on "The World This Weekend" the Sunday after the London rallies. It was an almost incoherent broadcast, giving the impression that the whole rally had been a series of interruptions to the accompaniment of deafening noise. Protests were made to the BBC by, among others, Peter Thompson, Eddy Stride and Lord Longford. As a result an informal enquiry was held into the broadcast by the BBC after which an apology was made, and it became known that several knuckles were rapped internally. Through Thompson's efforts an arrangement was made for Peter Hill to be interviewed on the PM Current Affairs programme.

Apart from the "personal appearances" of Malcolm Muggeridge, Mary Whitehouse, Cliff Richard and Peter Hill on news magazines and religious programmes on and around September 25, the major television coverage of the Festival had to wait nearly two months after the inaugural events for the Northern Festival of Light at Manchester on November 5 (an event virtually ignored by the national press, even in most of their northern editions). After weeks of patient and careful contact between Thompson and the *24 Hours* programme they decided to take film of the event for subsequent screening. Out of the three to four hours of film shot a very fair selection was made for a subsequent *24 Hours* programme report on the event which in ten minutes succeeded in representing some of the real issues which the Festival stood for and identifying the type of person most closely connected with the demonstration. But it is a matter of some amazement that the media did not take up the positive story of the Festival earlier.

What went wrong with the media coverage? Can it really be argued that a demonstration which drew, at a conservative estimate, 60,000 people to London from all parts of the country, was only as newsworthy as the demonstrations and other unrelated incidents appeared to make it? Has any comparable rally of similar size and significance in the field of unemployment, nuclear disarmament, race relations or other social issues ever had so distorted and inadequate a coverage in the major national newspapers?

Gavin Reid came very near to the point in an article about the Festival's inaugural press conference. He wrote in *CEN:* "The press folk had already worked out their story-line before they came—this was an anti-porn reactionary bonanza. Whenever the two 'stars' (Malcolm Muggeridge and Trevor Huddleston) spoke the camera was on but when a Danish Christian stood up to give a few home truths about what was happening in his country someone had to push his way through from the back to nudge the camera crew into recording that also. They had obviously worked out what would be worth listening to before the show had started. It all confirmed what the Leicester University study, 'Demonstrations and Communication', disturbingly revealed—that the newsmen tend to gather the news that supports their preconceived ideas".

It is not a question of the Festival organizers wanting a good press, though perhaps their protests at the coverage they received have unfortunately tended to give this impression. What they wanted, and what they had every right to expect, was fair coverage of their events and an adequate representation of their views on the issues with which they were concerned. Leaving aside all the difficulties that may have surrounded the earlier press relations policy of the Festival, the media in general, and the national newspapers in particular, must stand condemned for their inadequate reporting of the Festival. When asked by one of the Festival organizers what he knew about the Festival of Light an ordinary man in the street replied, "Isn't it something to do with mice and people dressed up as nuns?" No comment.

Chapter Eight

DIM RELIGIOUS LIGHT

To say that the Christian Church as a whole in Britain reacted with spontaneous enthusiasm to the Festival of Light would be a substantial overstatement. There was certainly a positive response from the evangelical constituency within the Anglican and Baptist Churches, together with those of Brethren and Pentecostal persuasion, but the official leadership of the mainstream denominations reacted with marked coolness with the notable exception of several Anglican Bishops. Letters were sent to denominational headquarters three months before the Festival explaining its aims and intentions and particularly seeking support for the Nationwide Day of Prayer, but there was little response from church leaders. To be fair it must be said that most of the denominations are structured in such a way as to make it difficult for them to commend a movement such as the Festival to their members even if they had wanted to. But many people will have echoed the sentiments of "Marksman", outspoken columnist of the *British Weekly* when he wrote the day before the Festival:

"I just don't know whether the denominations as such were invited to share in the Festival. If they were, and offered the standard knee-jerk response to anything not emanating from the British Council of Churches, I should be even more fed-up. But what I am most fed-up about is the apparent failure, over the post-war decades, of mainstream leadership to come up with anything (the Methodist Association of Youth Clubs' London Weekend apart) alive, relevant, potentially appealing in terms of mass response by young people in particular, within what you might call the field of contemporary Christian witness and evangelism.

"My growing feeling is that today's mainstream leadership is impeccably cerebral and minimally visceral. It seems at times possessed of all the passionless clarity of a telephone answering service.

"John Wesley had a strangely warmed heart allied to a strangely cool head. The latter, on its own, will always find deeply convincing reasons for playing it safe, remaining open-ended, instituting a dialogue, exploring in depth, setting up a commission, running a pilot scheme, circulating a paper, doing some research—in fact anything rather than go out on to the streets of Jerusalem drunk with the Spirit, and showing others how."

If the published reactions of some of the leaders of the British Council of Churches is anything to go by his remarks were not out of place. Bishop Kenneth Sansbury, its general secretary, addressing the Welsh Council of Churches in October, said the Festival had been used to mount "another evangelical campaign". Many Christians and other people concerned with the permissive society had been put off the campaign by the "old style revivalist" tone. While the organizers might have had strong feelings about the spread of pornography and permissiveness in society, he said, they had used the Festival for rather different purposes. "I recognize the initiative of these people but the way they have done this has not made it any easier for other Christians to join in."

His predecessor, Dr. Kenneth Slack, now minister of the City Temple, speaking at the BCC's half-yearly meeting later the same month, criticized the attitude to human sexuality adopted by some of those involved in the Festival.

Many took a positive line but there were perhaps one or two who most fully gained the attention of the mass media whose attitude to the flesh was "Manichaean to say the least".

The religious weekly press made up for any dilly-dallying by the denominational leadership by giving widespread coverage to the Festival in its news columns, its editorials and its correspondence columns. The news reports were generally objective, detailed, and with a few painful exceptions, accurate. Editorial opinions were generally favourable, though with some reservations, the least critical support coming, perhaps, from the Roman Catholic papers. But it was in the correspondence columns that the most interesting discussion took place, by far the most stimulating sequence of letters appearing in the *Church Times.* Sharply critical contributions from Miss Valerie Pitt, the Rev. Kenneth Leech and the Rev. Paul Oestreicher, matched by spirited replies from less well-known members of the Church of England kept the correspondence going until well into November.

Opposition to the Festival came from sources outside the Church as well as from within. The main areas of concern, repeated many times by different people in different places tended to revolve around a few basic issues which can probably best be summarized in the form of questions and answers.

Why concentrate on pornography when there are the much greater obscenities of homelessness, poverty, racialism, violence and so on? Bishop Trevor Huddleston answered this criticism several times during the course of his involvement with the Festival, pointing out that simply to protest against one form of obscenity did not mean either that one tolerated other forms of obscenity or that one was any less concerned about them than other people. Someone suggested to the Festival organizers the analogy of shooting birds in a tree. "Aim at the tree and you'll probably miss the birds; aim at one bird and you may hit it." The Festival aimed first at pornography, but it is not committed to protest only on that issue for the rest of its life. Initially that was the field in which it chose to work but even in the course of those early weeks it was dealing with other concerns.

Having said that, however, there is an important distinction which needs to be made about pornography in relation to other obscenities. Pornography is essentially a *product.* Homelessness and poverty are conditions, and racialism and violence are attitudes. Of course there are people with a vested interest in the continuation of situations in which the attitudes and conditions are maintained. But people are not being exploited as products in a multi-million pound business transaction. Furthermore, poverty, homelessness, racialism and violence are inherently evil; pornography is a distortion of something which is pure and good. As each young person develops to full sexual maturity he has to face up to this distortion for himself, whereas he may, by his background and circumstances, be shielded from the other obscenities referred to. Where they share common ground with pornography is in their tendency to dehumanize and devalue the dignity of man, but in other ways they are quite different, and should not be lumped together as part of the common problems facing mankind capable of direct comparison.

The evils of pornography may be great but surely the evils of censorship are greater? It has been truly said that we live in a more repressive society now than did our Victorian forefathers. Our freedom of action has been curtailed in almost every sphere other than those of culture and the arts, in the belief that the right to individual freedom must be dependent on the good of the whole community not being put at risk. We are not free to pay our taxes voluntarily because that would place the burden of taxation only on honest people. We are not free to pollute the atmosphere in certain areas with coal fires or untreated industrial fumes, because of the danger to the health and well-being of the community. If it is held that the publication or broadcasting of certain material will similarly put the well-being of the community at risk it is entirely logical and consistent to advocate that steps should be taken to prevent such material being disseminated.

The difficulty comes with defining what material is likely to put the community at risk. The few who take the extremist view that there should be complete freedom to present any type of material for public consumption have to follow the logic of that argument by opposing the Race Relations Act, the Obscene Publications Act, and even, presumably, the laws governing libel and slander. Whilst honouring the integrity of those who hold that view it must be said that it is neither widely held nor could it ever be an acceptable basis for the maintenance of a stable society. Most people accept that there is a need for some restraint in material relating to race relations, obscenity, national security and other sensitive areas. What the Festival of Light has done is to test public acceptance of present standards in relation to these matters and express the opinion that present laws relating to some of these issues should be strengthened.

What evidence is there that pornography does harm to anybody? Isn't it better to lift all the restrictions on pornography and people will become bored with it? Evidence in this field is very elusive, as it is in the fields of penology, exposure to violence, homelessness and many other areas. It is easy to see certain direct effects in relation to some of these evils: one harmful effect of poverty is unequal opportunity; a broken home has the effect of making a small child unstable. This cause and effect relationship cannot be scientifically proved, but there is sufficient circumstantial evidence to justify the assumption. The same can be said of pornography. Whilst the actual evidence of a link between pornography and someone committing rape or murder may be very small (though it does exist), it is a perfectly reasonable proposition that widespread acceptance of the values on which pornography is based would have the effect of breaking up the stability of family life and reducing human sexual relationships below those of animals. Judgement on the second point can only be a matter of opinion until further evidence is available from Denmark, where, as is well known, restrictions on pornography have been lifted. The views of the two Danes who came over for the Festival of Light have already been noted. One thing is clear. Although prohibition inevitably produces a "forbidden fruit" situation it is quite fatuous to argue that to remove all restrictions will automatically reduce the demand. The end of rationing after the last war had quite the reverse effect.

The Church has always had a thing about sex. Isn't it the case that those who have organized the Festival simply have some sort of sexual hang-up themselves, and are seeking to expunge their guilt by organizing the Festival? Bishop Trevor Huddleston's comment in this context has not been widely enough noted. He spoke of chastity as always having been in the forefront of the Church's teaching. True, it is but one of many virtues which the Church is called upon to preach, and it should not be given greater emphasis than honesty, unselfishness, compassion and the many other elements in the teaching of Jesus. The curious thing is that whilst there are many perfectly happy for the Church to encourage those beyond its bounds to be unselfish, honest, compassionate and so on, they seem to react violently at any suggestion that they should be chaste.

The biblical view of sex is that it is essentially positive that sexual relationships are primarily for companionship rather than procreation, and that nudity and love play in the context of a faithful relationship are noble and pure. This has been misinterpreted over the years by the Church partly through the false separation of spiritual and material. The Christian view of the importance of sexual morality in society is clearly based on the fact that it involves everyone at some stage of their lives and until comparatively recently was inextricably bound up with the procreation of human life, which the Bible, not alone, views with the greatest degree of seriousness.

So far as the Festival organizers and their own attitudes to sexuality and pornography are concerned it should be emphasized that, contrary to much that has been said and written, those involved have had interests far removed from this particular subject over many years. Eddy Stride is rector of a church in East London which runs a crypt ministry for the rehabilitation of vagrant alcoholics. Colonel

Dobbie is general secretary of the Southwark Council of Social Service, in which position he has had to fight for the needs of the underprivileged and deprived. Steve Stevens was for three years a pilot in the tricky and dangerous terrain of the Southern Sudan risking his life many times over for the sake of those who needed hospital treatment unobtainable by any means other than airlifting them out. Malcolm Muggeridge has capped a long and distinguished career as a writer and journalist with the incredible personal feat of raising over £100,000 for the needs of Pakistan refugees in India, and has given to Mother Theresa of Calcutta several thousand pounds of royalties from his book about her work among the destitute. Both Lord Longford and Peter Thompson have been heavily committed to the cause of penal reform and rehabilitation of ex-prisoners. Many others of those serving as members of the Council of Reference, the executive committee or as regional co-ordinators have given practical demonstrations of their concern for human need and deprivation in many varied spheres.

It is simply not true to say that they have one-track minds or that they have been lifelong crusaders against pornography. Many have been extremely reluctant to become involved because of the horror of appearing prudish, negative and censorious. They are men and women in public and private life who have been made aware of a common concern for the maintenance of standards of morality in public life conducive to the greatest good of the community as they see it.

Surely by drawing attention to these things by public protests and so on you are simply doing a disservice to your cause. Would it not be better to work behind the scenes? One of the purposes of the Festival of Light was to test the public reaction to a stand being taken on these issues. Had the Festival never taken place those concerned would never have known the extent to which they had any recognizable body of public opinion behind them. They deliberately chose the way of a national protest as a political demonstration of the support they anticipated they would get. Having persuaded a representative number of the "silent majority" to stand up and be counted they can now seek by careful diplomacy and rational discussion to encourage those in positions of responsibility in the government and the media to take action on the issues with which they are concerned.

Is there not a danger that in the present growing atmosphere of repression the Festival of Light will be increasingly identified with authoritarian bodies and movements whose ideals are far removed from those of Christ? There is certainly a danger that the Festival of Light may be identified with the National Front, or other neo-fascist movements, because they take a similar stand on these issues. They may even be infiltrated by those who wish to see a return to an authoritarian pattern of life and feel that support for the Festival and its objectives will be one way of achieving that. Someone has characterised this fear as the equivalent of seeing a fascist in every pew just as a few years ago a lot of people were accused of seeing a red under every bed, but there is a serious issue here and one which the Festival of Light organizers have said that they recognize.

In one of the subsequent demonstrations in which the Festival was involved, namely, the communion service at St. Paul's Cathedral in December 1971 when the cast of the musical *Hair* were taking part in celebration of the third anniversary of the show, the Christians who were protesting at the service outside St. Paul's were accompanied by National Front demonstrators with racist banners, thus giving the impression to the casual observer that the two demonstrations had a single mind. Trevor Huddleston has again contributed helpfully in this respect by pointing out that on several occasions he has shared a platform on the race issue with those of quite different political and ideological persuasions to himself, but that this was a risk he was prepared to take.

Did the Festival organizers not make a tactical error in lumping together the various unconnected groups who had been advocating freer attitudes to nudity and sexual behaviour? It is quite true that those who have been responsible for worsening standards of public morality are poles apart both in ideology and philosophy. It is difficult to say which are the more dangerous, the young idealists, who are sincerely sickened by the hypocrisy and injustice of contemporary society and are taking action which many find offensive to change the situation, or the cynical businessmen—and their shareholders—who exploit human weakness in their newspapers and magazines, careful to remain within the law and anxious to preserve the structure of a society which pays them a handsome dividend. Both groups are dangerous but for quite different reasons, and it was certainly a mistake to attack them both on the same front. Having said that it must be emphasized that those involved in, for instance, the underground press, against which the Festival of Light strictures have been particularly strong, are using pornography to further their political ends in the same way that capitalist pornographers further their business interests. For this reason, if for no other, they cannot blame the Festival organizers seeing them as hard-core porn pedlars.

Should Christians work with others against moral pollution? Eddy Stride sought to answer this question in an article sent to ministers and others by the Festival organizers. He drew his inspiration from the witness of Lord Shaftesbury and William Wilberforce in the previous century and pointed out that these men, though evangelical Christians, achieved notable reforms in respect of the abolition of the slave trade and the improvement of working conditions for women and children by virtue of the fact that they were in politics and mobilized opinion both inside and outside the church to strengthen their case. "If there is a problem with the drains or some other local health hazard, one would expect to find Christians of all persuasions standing with those of no religious conviction to get the health hazard put right. Big moral and social issues have commonly united people of various points of view in the past just as when our country went to war people ceased to stress their important differences and stressed rather their common concern for victory. There are reasons for believing that moral pollution is a threat to the survival of society equal to that facing us in wartime. We see a need to stand together with all men of goodwill against the concerted attack of our young people and older people too in the realm of morality and family life."

Why was the Festival of Light virtually monopolized by conservative evangelicals when the Council of Reference contained churchmen of other persuasions? The first working party was drawn from the evangelical constituency of the Anglican and Baptist Churches, together with those of Brethren and Pentecostal affiliation. This was not surprising in view of the fact that Peter Hill came from this background, as did most of those with whom he made his initial contacts. But there was an immediate concern on the part of some on the committee, notably Eddy Stride, that neither the Council of Reference nor the constituency from which support was requested should be exclusively evangelical in content. This decision was to earn them strong criticism from the extreme separatist group of Independent Evangelicals. Later as contacts were made throughout the country in search of regional co-ordinators it was to the evangelical constituency that most of the approaches were made and from which the most positive response came. There is evidence that in some cases evangelicals acted unilaterally in an area when it would have been possible and preferable to promote the Festival on a broader base. But time was often against the wider sharing of responsibility for local action and it was a case of "act now, talk later". The crowds who came to the events were by no means solidly evangelical. Many Roman Catholics turned out, for example, including *genuine* nuns!

Chapter Nine

REFLECTED LIGHT

The Nationwide Festival of Light began, as we have seen, with the vision of one man, who was prepared to act decisively on what he had seen. In so doing he set off a chain reaction amongst those who had been aware of the situation and had been acting independently for some time but without any coordination. But it is not quite as simple as that. Peter Hill's vision gave him no clear indication of what was to be achieved by "marching for Christ". It was apparent to those who took part in early discussions with him about the Festival that he had difficulty in "verbalizing the vision", and it seems reasonably certain that at the time he first received the vision he did not connect it with a protest against moral pollution. That came later as he talked with those who were particularly concerned about it. As the original working party grew into the executive committee this lack of clarity about aims and objects became more apparent, and certainly the dual "social involvement/evangelistic" thrust which resulted has given rise to some confusion and criticism.

Many of those who supported the Festival saw moral pollution as *evidence* that society was sinful and needed the preaching of the gospel. Others—men like Eddie Stride—while completely agreeing with this analysis held that because Christians were called upon to be the "salt of the earth" it was important to tackle the moral pollution *in itself*. They believed that in tackling such a target they would find allies from outside the churches and of other faiths. Throughout the planning and conduct of the Festival the two viewpoints were never fully resolved but on the other hand they existed together in a remarkably friendly tension.

The Trafalgar Square rally was criticized in *Crusade* magazine along these lines: here was a public meeting to deal with a social problem hoping for support from a wide section of the community but turning out to be a cheerful, youthful J-E-S-U-S chanting gospel demo. In other words the aim of evangelism crushed the sister aim of social action.

The truth is first that the platform cannot be blamed for the *appearance* of the crowd—it stuck to its brief. Secondly, however, appearances were deceptive. In fact there was a remarkably wide cross-section of age and most of those older people present were clear about the purpose of the rally. If there is a criticism, perhaps it lies in the fact that those nurturing the younger generation of Christians have not presented it with a big enough biblical perspective.

It would not be accurate to suggest that the Trafalgar Square crowd truly represented a cross-section of British society. They were obviously almost all committed Christians—mainly drawn from the evangelical tradition. Nevertheless every popular movement usually has been spearheaded by a small group of activists and the huge volume of mail received at the Festival office together with the remarkable support for the beacons lends some credence to the *Sunday Telegraph*'s claim that in the Festival of Light the silent majority had found—*its voice*.

Certainly those who actively opposed the Festival could not, and probably would not, claim to represent the majority of British people!

There were sound theological reasons for the dual aims of the Festival and it would be a tragedy if, in the future, the impetus behind one aim was to become greater at the expense of the other. The future struggle with moral pollution, however, must move away from the inevitable simplicity of rallies, demonstrations and slogans to the hard unglamorous grind of study, discussion, representation, and dialogue. Already some supporters of the Festival are engaged in just such activities. One wonders, however, how many of the demonstrating thousands have since taken up the Festival's challenge to talk to their local newsagents when blatantly pornographic material is openly displayed.

The fact that some of those who planned and mobilized the Festival were drawn from the Charismatic movement should not go unnoticed. This movement has been a growing force within the evangelical tradition and has indeed spilled over with an infectious enthusiasm into other sections of the Church.

They could be criticized, no doubt, as over-enthusiastic simplicists. It is very doubtful however if any other section of the Church would have had the quality of faith to attempt a "nationwide" project in the space of a few months on the basis of one man's vision, with no organization and no assured finance. On the other hand the tasks that lie ahead, particularly in the field of social action, will require something more than J-E-S-U-S chants and will call for the gift of wisdom as well as the gift of faith.

In contrast the failure of any denomination to come—as a body—to any clear position (for or against) the Festival is disturbing if not wholly surprising. One can only hope that the Festival movement and its aims in the future will draw a much wider support from the official structures of the Church.

What, then, are we to make of the Nationwide Festival of Light? To some of those involved in the Festival that is an impertinent question. They feel that it was "so obviously organized by God", to quote one letter-writer, that any judgement of man would not only be irrelevant but irreverent. But in fact some judgement must be made, and in the last analysis each person must come to their own judgement in the light of the facts as here related and their own experience of the Festival. The judgement of this book is that despite its admitted short-comings, weaknesses and at times wrong emphases (which no attempt has been made to conceal) the Festival of Light was a timely and necessary manifestation of the presence of God. As the story is traced through from Peter Hill's original vision to the great Trafalgar Square and Hyde Park rallies one is aware, as those most intimately concerned with the Festival were aware, of divine direction and control. This is not an arrogant, exclusive claim. Of course God works in many and various ways in His world, often when those concerned are least aware. But it is all too easy for a mass movement to gain momentum and fire the imagination entirely through human endeavour and natural circumstances.

Human endeavour was indeed evident throughout the Festival, seldom can so much work have been done by so few in so short a time. Natural circumstances were undoubtedly propitious; both the timing, with the *Oz* trial and the *Little Red School Book* fresh in people's minds, and the manner, capitalizing quite legitimately on the outward manifestations of the Jesus People, were superb. But there was a plus factor. How else can one explain the smooth functioning of so diverse a committee, the availability at just the right time of premises and staff adequate—just—for the felt needs of the moment, the provision of facilities at Hyde Park and elsewhere when humanly speaking there seemed little hope? Identification of this "plus factor" may vary. To one it may be that the Festival "sprang up from the grass roots and was watered by the Holy Spirit". Another will rightly point to "the vast army of people" who prayed for the Festival whilst to someone else it will be put down as "a wonderful experience of the sovereign moving of God in grace".

To this writer it seems to have been a mixture of all three —and a further demonstration, if such were needed, that God works through people. But let Gordon Landreth of the executive committee have the last word—"It is God who has been at work and we want Him to have the glory!"

POSTSCRIPT

The Festival of Light did not end on September 25. There was an understandable pause to take stock of the situation following the climactic events at Trafalgar Square and Hyde Park before the executive committee came to a firm decision to continue. They only do so, in Peter Hill's words, because of "the overwhelming response from the local churches and areas throughout the country", and further serious consideration of the pros and cons of setting up "yet another organization" in the already crowded evangelical scene. A permanent staff of four was appointed, including the two honorary secretaries, to co-ordinate future plans. The Council of Reference and executive committee were retained together with a national committee comprising the Executive Committee, the original co-ordinators and co-opted members.

Follow-up of the September rallies took various forms: copies of the appropriate Trafalgar Square proclamations were delivered personally to 10 Downing Street, BBC and

ITA headquarters and Church House; printed leaflets containing the full text of all three were mailed to every member of the House of Commons and the House of Lords and to regional supporters for their local civic leaders; Northern and Scottish Festivals of Light were held in Manchester and Glasgow; support was given to the protest against the "Hair" Communion Service at St. Paul's Cathedral and to Mary Whitehouse's National Petition for Public Decency; numerous meetings have been addressed, conferences held and correspondence answered; a Christmas campaign based on the theme "*Christ*mas—the Festival of Light" including torchlight carol services was held in several major cities and large towns the weekend before Christmas 1971, with posters, car stickers and Christmas cards emphasizing the theme.

Plans for future activities are still being finalized at the time of writing but for 1972 they include an extensive programme of local activities with teams of Christians speaking up and down the country teaching the aims of the Festival, culminating in a series of regional Gospel Festivals. A four-day long London Festival is planned for the summer involving concerts, street preaching and personal evangelism, together with Bible teaching and prayer fellowship for those participating. Finally there will be an augmented Christmas programme following the 1971 pattern only on a much larger scale. On the more specifically moral pollution front, meetings are planned between Festival representatives and leading figures in the government and media. Local supporters are being urged to act by taking part in "Operation Newsagent", a co-ordinated effort to persuade newsagents to reconsider their policy on stocking and displaying pornographic magazines, putting pressure on local film licensing committees, tackling their MPs and prospective candidates about their views on moral pollution and generally being "salt in society". All in all, it very much looks as if the 1971 Festival of Light was but the springboard for a much more ambitious and far-reaching effort in 1972.